SOUTHAMPTON'S QUAYSIDE STEAM

Dave Marden

Kestrel Railway Books
PO Box 269
SOUTHAMPTON
SO30 4XR

www.kestrelrailwaybooks.co.uk

Printed by the Amadeus Press.

ISBN 978-1-905505-02-9

Front cover: Destined to be the last of its class, E1 No 32694 shunts an early duo of container wagons at the Western Docks in April 1960. (Colour Rail)

Back cover, top: Class C14 as BR No 30589 at the Town Quay, Southampton. (M.H. Walshaw)

Back cover, bottom: One of McAlpine's locos with a train of soil heads off across the works site that afterwards became Mayflower Park, during construction of the Western Docks. (Associated British Ports)

Dedication

This book is dedicated to the memory of my parents.

Contents

Introduction

Having been born in the Chapel area of Southampton, I spent my formative years surrounded by the sights and sounds of the local industrial landscape. To the south were the Docks, while the town gas works sat like huge dark shadow to the north. To the east was the River Itchen with its wharves, while the original London and Southampton Railway ran down to the Terminus station on the west side to complete the enclosure.

Apart from trips to London when visiting relatives, I had little early interest in railways, especially those of an industrial nature, and although I lived just a few hundred yards from the Chapel Tramway, I never really gave it much thought. It was just a part of the local scene, being at best a curiosity, and at worst a minor inconvenience when it held me up in Melbourne Street on my way to school.

My memory of Marine Parade in the 1950s recalls that the track running alongside the roadway appeared to be in a fairly perilous state, being quite buckled and twisted with compacted coal dust up to the top of the rails. The train would lurch and squeal along its way to the various wharves, defying the odds by staying on course and avoiding derailment. Some of the hand-operated points had fallen into disuse with their prostrate levers embedded in the grime at ground level. The actual roadway alongside at this point was fairly narrow, and collisions with vehicles were not unknown.

Eventually, my enthusiasm for railways developed, but it was strictly limited to main line traffic. Northam station was a regular "after-school" haunt for the sighting of Western Region "Halls" and "Granges" on the Portsmouth to Cardiff service, and my first glimpses of the "Bull's Run" were from that station, where the double track ran from a point under the railway bridge, and curved away south eastwards before disappearing behind a gas holder. My friends and I would occasionally spot industrial 0-4-0 saddle tanks hauling trains of hopper wagons laden with coal in the direction of Dibles Wharf. Of course, these weren't "real" trains, but they did have a certain attraction and, as curiosity took over, we began to investigate this mystery line.

A stroll round to Britannia Road revealed the other end of the curved track with which we had become familiar from our vantage point at Northam station; here it crossed the road and headed eastwards towards the River Itchen. Another crossing over Belvedere Road saw the line disappear through the gates of Corralls yard. It was a while before we ventured inside and asked to look around at the busy scene where rails seemed to run everywhere and a Peckett saddle tank named *Bristol* stood invitingly at centre stage. A preliminary chat to the driver brought forth an invitation to step up into the cab for a short journey across the yard, and from that moment I was sold on industrial locos.

As steam began to give way to diesel, the only pockets of resistance seemed to be those industrial lines that I had ignored for so long, and an earnest quest began to see what I had missed. From that time onwards, I became a regular visitor to the wharves and quaysides around me.

Although I didn't realise it at the time, there was another equally interesting tramway nearby, which ran from just south of the Mount Pleasant level crossing. I had observed the occasional train trundling between the buildings of the Southern Television studios and disappearing under Northam Road Bridge, before emerging on the other side and rattling out of sight along Drivers Wharf.

As the steam era neared its end with the wholesale scrapping of main line steam, it was possible to see wagon loads of cut-up BR locos making slow progress through Drivers Wharf on their way to Pollock and Brown's scrapyard at Northam. It was a macabre pastime trying to spot a severed cab-side number and discover the identity of the torched victim.

I arrived at the Town Quay offices of Southampton Harbour Board in 1963, as a skinny, naive fifteen year old, to begin my working career. At that time, rail traffic was very much in evidence with the local shunter assembling wagons on the seafront sidings for the daily freight collection. In those days, the main commodity was timber, imported via a continuous flow of coasters from Scandinavia. Apart from the Town Quay rail traffic, there were constant movements along the line that connected the Eastern and Western Docks and, during my school years, I had often spent time at the nearby Mayflower Park where USA tanks would pass at frequent intervals travelling in either direction. During my first few weeks working for the SHB, I must have spent a great deal of my time gazing out of the windows at passing trains whenever loud rumblings signalled their approach.

The docks always held a fascination for me, as I grew up on their doorstep during my childhood, adolescence and early adulthood. Many of my relatives worked in port-related industries or sailed in the ships, so I had a good knowledge of what was there before I had even ventured inside the gates. As teenagers, my friends and I would make frequent visits to the docks running shed and, apart from the regular collection of USA and E class tanks assembled, there always seemed to be something new each time we called. Entry to the docks was provided through devious means – by obtaining a fishing permit at the pass office (a wooden hut facing onto Canute Road). This cost nothing, and the fact that we entered the gates without any visible fishing tackle hardly seemed to bother anyone. On the rare occasions when we were challenged, we were "meeting up with our fellow anglers who were already in there".

Having spent my formative working years at the Harbour Board, I was transferred to the Docks Board in 1968. At that time, the docks were railway orientated and the entire estate was dotted with countless wooden cabins for the accommodation of shunting crews, linesmen, and an army of flagmen guarding the myriad of road crossings. Indeed, there seemed to be a railway connected building every few yards. Many of the huts originally contained a coal-burning stove, but most had been replaced by electric heaters and Baby Belling cookers. These were small electric table top ovens, roughly the size of a large microwave, but in winter time their prime purpose appeared to be in heating the accommodation by having all the elements burning away continuously for 24 hours a day!

Eling was "The Port of Totton" according to a friend who lived there. Road journeys over the causeway had offered glimpses of the rails around the premises of the South Western Tar Distilleries, including the occasional sighting of a working saddle tank from Burt, Boulton & Haywood. Thus, the Eling Tramway was fully investigated, and entry to the tar works yard was soon granted. *Benton II* stood simmering in front of its shed, as the engineer told us there was not much call for its services because trade from vessels calling at the wharf had virtually ceased. Soon, any shunting around the works would be performed by one of several steam rail cranes in use there and *Benton II* would be cut up.

I was blissfully unaware of any railway operation at the former Woolston Rolling Mills when, as a teenager, I occasionally used to fish off the jetty (until being escorted off the premises by the Royal Navy security guards). To be honest, it was for my own safety as the wooden structure was in particularly poor condition with rotting timbers and large gaps in the decking. Only during comparatively recent years did I notice that some local maps indicated the presence of track at the seaward end of the depot. This of course, had long since been lifted by the time I diced with the authorities there.

The town (now city) of Southampton was never over-blessed with industrial railways, at least, not in the sense of those required by heavy industries, engineering or manufacturing complexes, but there were a few, and most of those that did exist served the seaborne trades of the docks and river wharves. The object of this book is to illustrate, and pay tribute to, the surprising number of steam workhorses that served so well over many generations.

My purpose is to focus upon the inconspicuous steam locomotives that laboured, largely unobserved, around the hidden sheds and yards of Southampton's quaysides. Not for them the glory of heading prestige boat trains to famed ocean liners, or hauling immense goods trains to Nine Elms and beyond. Theirs was the backstage role without which the main line stars would not have shone, and I hope this insight to their humble past will portray the true value of their huge supporting role.

During my researches I found that much information on this subject had been previously covered by a host of publications but, in almost all cases, as individual items, and in a less comprehensive form over a long timescale. However, I have not attempted to produce a meticulous reference work, but endeavoured to collate these records and wherever possible, add to them, creating an overall picture of the lines and the shunting locomotives that made up Southampton's Quayside Steam.

Dave Marden, Southampton 2007.

Acknowledgments

In compiling this book, the author wishes to thank all those who have generously offered their time and knowledge in helping to answer the countless queries that have arisen. If errors have occurred, it is in all probability that the author has misinterpreted their invaluable input.

Special thanks must go to the members of the Industrial Locomotive Society, the Industrial Railway Society, and the staff at the Southampton City Archive, whose individual and collective help has been immeasurable. Mention must also be made of the South Western Circle members and local historian, Bert Moody, whose enthusiasm and encouragement has been a great incentive, and finally to Ivor Thomas, librarian of the IRS whose assistance is greatly appreciated.

Many of the photographs in this book have been provided by the above organisations and individuals, or are taken from the author's collection, which has accumulated over many years with the assistance of friends, colleagues and associates, but in some cases their origins have been forgotten or obscured by time. Where the sources are known, the author has given due credit and made reasonable efforts to contact the photographers to seek permission for their use, but if I have inadvertently overlooked anyone, wrongly credited material, or unwittingly infringed anyone's copyright, please accept my sincerest apologies.

In conclusion, attention must be drawn of the large number of reference works studied during the course of writing, and in particular:

The various works of D.L. Bradley (RCTS)
The B4 Dock Tanks by Peter Cooper
The Story of the Southern USA Tanks by H. Sprenger, K. Robertson and C. Sprenger
Southampton's Railways by Bert Moody
The Train Ferries at Southampton by Fred Neill (South Western Circle)
The Industrial Locomotive and publications of the ILS
The Industrial Railway Record and numerous handbooks of the IRS
Making Tracks by J.R. Fairman
A History of RNSD Woolston by Joe Moore
The Story of the McAlpine Steam Locomotives by J.B. Latham

"Clausentum" at the Royal Pier terminus in the early 1900s. (Author's Collection)

CHAPTER 1

Southampton Dock Company 1842-1892

Because the Southampton Harbour Commissioners were unable to raise the necessary funding, the Southampton Dock Company was formed and authorised to construct the initial phase of the docks by Act of Parliament in 1836, with work commencing after the foundation stone had been laid some two years later. The main London to Southampton Railway was fully opened in 1840 and, following the completion of the initial dock (Outer dock - berths 1 to 9) in 1842, the quayside rails were connected to the Town (Terminus) Station.

Dry docks Nos 1 and 2 were constructed on the south side of the dock and opened in 1846 and 1847 respectively, following which the Inner dock (berths 10 to 19) was opened for business in 1851. A very much larger dry dock (No 3) was constructed alongside the others by 1854 and, as traffic increased, more power was eventually needed to cope with the growing volume of goods and materials in transit.

Initially, the docks system was operated by horses as far as the terminus exchange sidings, but by July 1865 the LSWR well tank *Crescent* had conducted steam trials over the docks lines. *Chaplin*, a small 0-4-0 vertical boilered tank engine, was built in 1861 by Alexander Chaplin of Glasgow, and the Dock Company acquired it second-hand from R. Brotherhood & Co of Chippenham in November 1865. It proved to be a worthwhile investment by allowing several horses and their teams to be disposed of, and with its greater working capacity, it proved an immediate success. So much so, that a second locomotive was quickly requested.

Osborne was ordered in June 1866 from Simpson and Co, who acted as agents for the manufacturer, Henry Hughes of Loughborough. While awaiting its delivery, the Dock Company gave a trial to a Manning Wardle tank engine, but returned it as "unsuitable" as soon as *Osborne* became available for duty following its arrival by sea in September that year. *Osborne* suffered some initial problems and to improve its performance several modifications were made, but it was never a great success and was regarded as a rather weak engine.

As demand increased still further, more motive power was called for, and a third locomotive was ordered in April 1870 from Dick and Stevenson of Airdrie. Arriving some three months later, *Canute,* an 0-4-0ST, was larger and more powerful than its predecessors, and within a year was carrying out duties mostly unaided with *Chaplin* worn out and *Osborne* reduced to a minor role.

The dock locos were originally housed in No 3 Berth Cargo Shed, which was adjacent to the company's marine workshops, but in August 1871 the Dock Company chairman announced a new "stable" had been provided for them. This was a purpose-built engine shed to the south of dry docks 1 and 2 which, subject to several later rebuilds, became the permanent motive power location until the docks rail system all but ceased in the 1970s.

Although *Chaplin* was subsequently patched up and

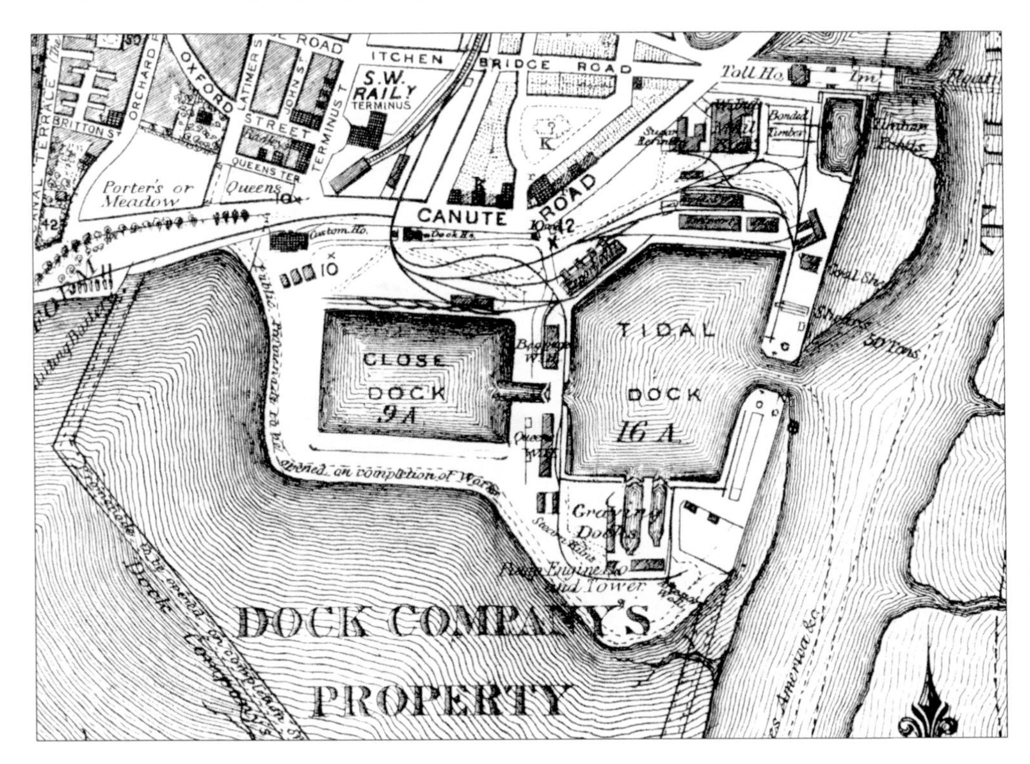

The docks in their earliest form in the 1850s showing the Inner (Close) and Outer (Tidal) docks, and the two dry docks. (From a Philip Brannon engraving)

pressed back into service, a fourth locomotive became a necessity, and an order was placed with Alexander Shanks and Son at Arbroath for an additional 0-4-0ST. Due to labour troubles at the manufacturer's works, *Sir Bevis* arrived three months late in January 1872, whereupon, *Chaplin* was sold to a second-hand locomotive dealer, J.M. Chester of Caernarvon, within days of its arrival.

Sir Bevis proved so successful that an identical engine was requested after just a few months. *Ascupart* was delivered in July 1872 and *Osborne* was immediately sold to J. Cowdy & Co of London, who were also agents of Henry Hughes and Co. It is probable that both *Chaplin* and *Osborne* were both sold on to new owners.

The capacities of the Inner and Outer docks were enhanced by extending the harbour southwards, and the new Itchen Quays (berths 30 to 33) were opened in 1875, with an additional dry dock (No 4) being opened in 1879.

The trio of *Canute*, *Sir Bevis* and *Ascupart* coped admirably for a few years until the locomotive stock needed to be increased once again, and another 0-4-0ST *Vulcan*, built by the Vulcan Foundry, at Newton-le-Willows in Lancashire, was delivered in August 1878. As with the previous order, this was followed almost immediately by a repeat order for a second engine named *Bretwalda*, which arrived for service during November that year.

During these years of great docks activity, the Dock Company took loan of a locomotive from the LSWR Engineering Department. This was a 2-4-0T named *Scott*, which was brought in to cover for a short period while one of the regulars was away under repair during 1888.

The building of the Empress dock (berths 20 to 28, opened in 1890), demanded yet another increase in the docks motive power when Hawthorn, Leslie & Co were given an order for two more 0-4-0ST locomotives. *Clausentum* and *Ironside* made their debuts in July 1890, once again following a delay at the maker's works. These were the biggest and best of all the dock locos to date, and were also the final engines purchased by the old Dock Company before it was taken over by the LSWR just two years later.

Warehouses D and E are prominent in this view of the Dock Company estate taken around 1890 from the roof of the South Western Hotel. Also visible at the bottom left of the picture are the rail connections across Canute Road to the Town (Terminus) Station. (Author's Collection)

Southampton Dock Company 0-4-0VBT *Chaplin*

Name:	*Chaplin*
Manufacturer:	Alexander Chaplin & Co Ltd, Glasgow
Built:	1861
Works number:	177
Cylinders:	8in x 14in
At the docks:	1865-1872

Chaplin was built in March 1861, and supplied new to Rowland Brotherhood & Co of Chippenham who had employed it on the construction of the Bristol and South Wales Union Railway. The Dock Company acquired it second-hand for £350 in November 1865 and, as their first steam locomotive, it was so successful that a second engine was soon demanded. However, as greater motive power became available, it found itself to be obsolete and, following the arrival of *Sir Bevis,* it was sold for £150 on 17th January 1872 to J.M. Chester of Caernarvon, who were dealers in second-hand locomotives. No further record is known, although Chester was advertising for sale a small 0-4-0T with vertical boiler and 8in cylinders just three months later.

Not "Chaplin" but a younger sister of 1871 vintage from the same builder gives an idea of its appearance. (B. Roberts)

Southampton Dock Company 0-4-0ST *Osborne*

Name:	*Osborne*
Manufacturer:	Henry Hughes & Co Ltd, Loughborough, Leicestershire
Built:	1866
Cylinders:	8½in x 15in
Driving wheels:	2ft 10in
Tank capacity:	200gal
Weight:	9ton 0cwt
At the docks:	1866-1872

Osborne was ordered through agents Simpson & Co of London, on behalf of the builders Henry Hughes, and arrived at the docks direct from Hughes in September 1866 at a cost of £600, replacing an on-loan Manning Wardle 0-4-0ST, and becoming the Dock Company's second purchased locomotive. *Osborne* was not a success. It had been constructed as an 0-4-0WT, and appears to have had several modifications carried out at the docks in order to improve its performance. But despite these, including the fitting of a 325 gallon saddle tank and larger 3ft 0in wheels, it was soon relegated to engineering works, and by 1872 had been put up for sale along with *Chaplin.* In July that year *Osborne* was purchased for £450 by J. Cowdy & Co of London, who were also agents for the builders, Hughes, and it is assumed the loco was refurbished and sold on to another owner, possibly on the continent.

Southampton Dock Company 0-4-0ST *Canute*

Name:	*Canute*
Manufacturer:	Dick & Stevenson, Airdrie
Built:	1870
Cylinders:	10in x 16in
Driving wheels:	3ft 2in
Tank capacity:	385gal
Weight:	11ton 15cwt
At the docks:	1870-1903

Canute arrived by sea from the makers on 12th July 1870, at a cost of £830 and, being much more powerful than either *Chaplin* or *Osborne*, it was an extremely well regarded engine, working trouble-free for long periods. Having carried out the bulk of docks duties almost single-handedly, it was practically rebuilt at the docks during 1878 when new cylinders, firebox, wheels and chimney were fitted. *Canute* entered LSWR stock in 1892, when the railway company purchased the docks, but the arrival of the first clutch of B4 tanks the following year saw its use decline until being used as a stationary boiler became its prime function. Its condition gradually deteriorated until it was finally taken out of service and broken up at the docks in October 1903.

Southampton Dock Company 0-4-0ST *Sir Bevis*

Name:	*Sir Bevis*
Manufacturer:	Alexander Shanks & Son, Arbroath
Built:	1871
Cylinders:	10in x 20in
Driving wheels:	3ft 0in
Wheelbase:	5ft 6in
Tank capacity:	325gal
Weight:	16ton 18cwt
At the docks:	1872-1903

Sir Bevis was built in 1871 at a cost of £840, and arrived in January 1872. It was the first of two locos purchased by the Dock Company from Shanks, the other being sister engine *Ascupart* which arrived a few months later. The pair worked on until the docks were acquired by the LSWR, and they became part of the railway company stock in 1892. However, following the arrival of the B4 tanks, both were steamed only occasionally, and were eventually offered for sale in January 1903. *Sir Bevis* was sold in March that year for £175 to C.D. Phillips of Newport, South Wales, who were advertising it for sale some two years afterwards as No 93 named *Emlyn*.

Southampton Dock Company 0-4-0ST *Ascupart*

Name:	*Ascupart*
Manufacturer:	Alexander Shanks & Son, Arbroath
Built:	1872
Cylinders:	10in x 20in
Driving wheels:	3ft 0in
Wheelbase:	5ft 0in
Tank capacity:	325gal
Weight:	16ton 18cwt
At the docks:	1872-1903

Ascupart was supplied new from the makers on 21st July 1872 following the success of sister engine *Sir Bevis*, which had arrived just a few months earlier. *Ascupart* worked on until becoming part of the LSWR stock when the railway company purchased the docks in 1892, but by then it was regarded only as a standby engine. 1893 saw the first arrival of the B4 class tanks, and the old Dock Company locomotives eventually became surplus to requirements. *Ascupart* and *Sir Bevis* were both withdrawn and offered for sale in January 1903, and *Ascupart* was last recorded as being shipped to Newcastle, New South Wales in Australia.

"Canute" in a dilapidated state pictured at the docks in 1901. (Roger Griffiths Collection)

"Sir Bevis" (right) and running mate "Canute" at the docks shed circa 1901. (Roger Griffiths Collection)

LSWR Engineering Department loco "Scott" pictured at Nine Elms (see page 8). (Author's Collection)

Southampton Dock Company 0-4-0ST *Vulcan*

Name:	*Vulcan*
Manufacturer:	Vulcan Foundry Ltd, Newton-le-Willows, Lancashire
Built:	1878
Works number:	836
Running numbers:	118, 111, 0111 (all LSWR)
Cylinders:	10in x 20in
Driving wheels:	3ft 0in
Working pressure:	120psi
Tank capacity:	350gal
Weight:	17ton 11½cwt
At the docks:	1878-1900

At a cost of £855, *Vulcan* arrived new from the builders in August 1878, and was so impressive that a sister engine *Bretwalda* was immediately ordered and supplied in November the same year. Both locos were adapted to carry emergency fire pumps on their front buffer beams when required. After being taken into LSWR stock in 1892, *Vulcan* was numbered 118 in December 1893, and was renumbered as 111 in July 1899. When replaced by the B4 class locos in April 1900, it was sent to Bournemouth for work as shed pilot and standby for Poole Quay, and within a year it had been joined there by former SDC running mate *Bretwalda*.

By April 1904, *Vulcan* had been again been renumbered, this time to 0111 and was then sent to work on the construction of the Bentley & Bordon Camp Light Railway, where it was reunited with another former SDC loco *Ironside*. The works were completed by December 1905, and the pair moved on to other duties between Brockenhurst and Pokesdown. Afterwards, *Vulcan* returned to the Southampton area around 1908, and worked there until being laid up at Eastleigh in October 1913. Following the outbreak of war, it was reprieved from the scrap heap to continue duties around Winchester and Southampton, from where it made an occasional visit to the Town Quay. In December 1917, it was sent to work on ballast trains during the construction of the new Feltham Yard. After the formation of the Southern Railway it was laid aside, but again reprieved in February 1924, when it was sold for £300 to E.E. Carnforth & Co of Stoke on Trent, who were acting on behalf of new owners Taylor, Tunnicliffe & Co at Stone in Staffordshire, where it worked until it was scrapped on site after being replaced in 1931.

Southampton Dock Company 0-4-0ST *Bretwalda*

Name:	*Bretwalda*
Manufacturer:	Vulcan Foundry Ltd, Newton-le-Willows, Lancashire
Built:	1878
Works number:	837
Running numbers:	408, 0408 (both LSWR), E0408 (SR)
Cylinders:	10in x 20in
Driving wheels:	3ft 0in
Working pressure:	120psi
Tank capacity:	350gal
Weight:	17ton 11½cwt
At the docks:	1878-1900

Bretwalda arrived new from the builders in November 1878 to join sister engine *Vulcan*, which was already at Southampton. Both locomotives were adapted to carry emergency fire pumps on their forward buffer beams when required. *Bretwalda* became part of LSWR stock when the docks were taken over by the railway in 1892, and remained there until being transferred to the Royal Pier service in April 1900 where, as No 408, it replaced Shanks loco *Ritzebuttel*. Its stay on the pier was short-lived, as by October the following year it was working at Bournemouth, and then at Winchester four months later. Afterwards, it returned to Eastleigh shed until it was loaned to the Engineer's Department as No 0408 in 1907 for work on the Exmouth to Topsham line.

Bretwalda was next employed in the building of the new railway works at Eastleigh, after which it was sent to Guildford as shed pilot until December 1910. There then came spells at Winchester and Fareham, with a brief return to Southampton's Town Quay before journeying on to Nine Elms in 1913. There, it resumed its role as shed pilot until moving back to Guildford the following year, where it remained until laid up in March 1924. By October that year it was back to work as No E0408, but by December 1925, its Southern Railway days were deemed over as it was put up for sale. Its eventual purchaser was J.R. Wood & Co at Dibles Wharf, Southampton in November 1926 (see Chapter 14). In December 1931, while at Eastleigh for overhaul, *Bretwalda* was temporarily replaced at Dibles by former docks stable mate *Ironside* and, thereafter, continued duties at Woods until scrapped in September 1935 by Pollock and Brown.

Dock Company locomotive "Vulcan" and crew pose for the camera during a quiet moment. (Author's Collection)

Southampton Dock Company loco "Bretwalda" at Guildford shed in the 1920s. (Bert Moody Collection)

LSWR Engineer's Department 2-4-0T *Scott*

Name:	*Scott*
Manufacturer:	George England & Co Ltd, London
Built:	1861
Running numbers:	15 (Engineer's Dept), 21, 021 (both LSWR)
Cylinders:	11in x 16in (11¼in x 16in after re-build)
Driving wheels:	3ft 10in (4ft 0in after rebuild)
Wheelbase:	10ft 0in
Weight:	17ton 0cwt
At the docks:	1888

Delivered new to the LSWR Engineer's Department in December 1861, *Scott* worked for many years at Wimbledon Permanent Way Depot until purchased by the locomotive department and sent to Cornwall in January 1874. When transferred back to Wimbledon in March 1886, it returned to the Engineer's Department stock. After a complete overhaul and rebuild, the loco was sent to work at Bournemouth, Salisbury, and then Northam in July 1888, and while at Northam was loaned to the Southampton Dock Company to cover for absentees under repair. *Scott* was later employed on the Lee-on-the-Solent line from April 1898, running as No 21 until scrapped in April 1909 as LSWR No 021.

See page 5 for an illustration of this locomotive.

Southampton Dock Company 0-4-0ST *Clausentum*

Name:	*Clausentum*
Manufacturer:	R. & W. Hawthorn, Leslie & Co Ltd, Newcastle-on-Tyne
Built:	1890
Works number:	2174
Running numbers:	457, 0457, 734 (all LSWR), E734 (SR)
Cylinders:	12in x 20in
Driving wheels:	3ft 2in
Wheelbase:	5ft 6in
Working pressure:	120psi
Tank capacity:	600gal
Weight:	21ton 2cwt
At the docks:	1890–1901

Clausentum was delivered new to the docks with sister engine *Ironside* at £985 apiece in July 1890, and these were the final two locos purchased by the Dock Company before it was taken over by the LSWR in 1892. Like all the Dock Company locomotives *Clausentum* eventually became surplus to requirements after the arrival of the B4 tanks, and it was transferred to the Royal Pier service, where it replaced Shanks loco *Cowes* in March 1901 as LSWR No 457. There, it rejoined former SDC running mate No 408 *Bretwalda*, and another Shanks engine *Southampton*, but the reunion lasted only until the following year when *Bretwalda* moved to Bournemouth.

Clausentum, shared duties with *Southampton* until becoming the Town Quay shunter in late 1906, when class C14 motor tanks took over at the Royal Pier. It became No 0457 in May 1908, and then No 734 from January 1914. Later that year, war service saw it loaned to the Government cordite factory at Holton Heath, near Wareham, after which it saw spells of employment at Hamworthy and Winchester, while rotating its Town Quay duties with C14 locos until, in Southern Railway days as No E734, it exchanged roles with *Ironside* as Guildford shed pilot in 1924. *Ironside* then took the occasional turn at the Town Quay.

Then followed another spell at Bournemouth, but by February 1928, it was back at Guildford where it remained until July 1936, when after repairs at Eastleigh it was placed in store. From then, it saw only occasional service as cover for the C14s at the Town Quay and Redbridge Sleeper Depot until being moved to Crayford, Kent in August 1939, and on to Fratton by March 1940, before its final allocation back as Guildford shed pilot until scrapped in August 1945.

See page 105 for an illustration of this locomotive.

Southampton Dock Company 0-4-0ST *Ironside*

Name:	*Ironside*
Manufacturer:	R. & W. Hawthorn, Leslie & Co Ltd, Newcastle-on-Tyne
Built:	1890
Works number:	2175
Running numbers:	458, 0458, (both LSWR), E0458 3458 (SR), 30458 (BR)
Cylinders:	12in x 20in
Driving wheels:	3ft 2in
Wheelbase:	5ft 6in
Working pressure:	120psi
Tank capacity:	600gal
Weight:	21ton 2 cwt
At the docks:	1890-1901

Ironside arrived new from the makers in July 1890 along with sister engine *Clausentum*, the pair being the last locomotives purchased by the Dock Company before being taken over by the LSWR. Although becoming part of the railway company stock in 1892, no number was allocated until, after being replaced by B4 tanks, *Ironside* was transferred to Bournemouth in March 1901 as No 458, where it resumed its partnership with former SDC running mate *Vulcan*.

After a spell of shunting in the Poole area *Ironside* was transferred to Eastleigh in April 1904. From there it was sent to construction works on the Pirbright Junction to Basingstoke line, before moving on to the Bordon & Bentley Camp Light Railway (completed December 1905), and finally for work on the Exmouth Junction to Topsham line in 1907. By the middle of 1908, it had returned to Bournemouth and was next located at both Southampton and Eastleigh Carriage Works (being renumbered 0458 in December 1912). In Southern Railway service it became E0458 upon replacing *Bretwalda* at Guildford in January 1926, where it remained for many years, apart from the occasional return to Bournemouth or Eastleigh. *Ironside* was renumbered 3458 in November 1931 and, in the following month, during a return to the Southampton area, was temporarily transferred to J.R. Wood & Co at Dibles Wharf, while former SDC stable mate *Bretwalda* was at Eastleigh for overhaul (see Chapter 14).

In April 1944, it was sent on loan to Stewarts Lane milk depot, and later in the year, was at Tonbridge and Brighton before completing a round trip to Guildford. There, upon nationalisation, it received its final identity as British Railways No 30458 and it remained there until being taken out of service in June 1954, being the last survivor of the old Dock Company locos. It was broken up at Eastleigh in September of that year.

SDC loco "Ironside" pictured in Southern Railway days at Eastleigh in 1923. (H.C. Casserley)

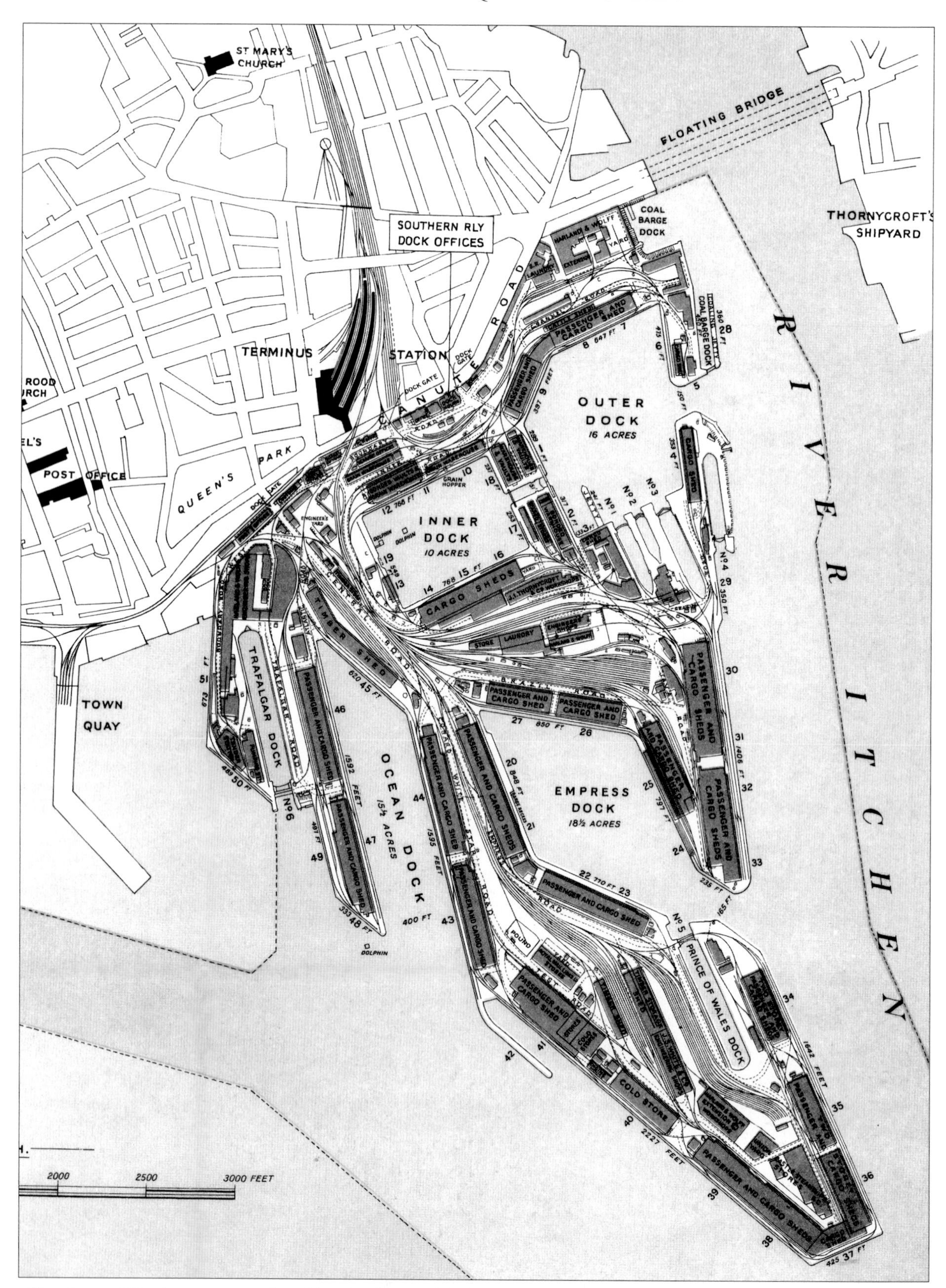

The Eastern Docks in its completed state.

CHAPTER 2

LSWR Docks 1892-1922

The Dock Company, being unable to raise sufficient finance to extend their facilities to cope with the fast expanding trade, finally succumbed to purchase by the LSWR in November 1892, and the new owners immediately set about utilising the full potential of their latest acquisition. Improvements to the docks continued with the completion of yet another dry dock, the Prince of Wales (No 5 in 1895, the biggest so far at 745ft long), together with new berths 34 to 36 (then known as the Prince of Wales Quays) and berths 37 to 42 (the Test Quays), which were all were completed by 1902. Finally, the Trafalgar Dry Dock (No 6), the biggest of all in the Eastern Docks at 912ft long, was opened for business by 1905.

Although permanently based in the docks, former Dock Company locos *Canute*, *Sir Bevis*, *Ascupart*, *Vulcan*, *Bretwalda*, *Clausentum* and *Ironside* became LSWR stock, but were not immediately allocated numbers, as responsibility for their maintenance was given to the Docks Department, formed to operate quite separately from the railway itself. Some of the earlier SDC locos were now beginning to show their age, and with trade growing still further under the new railway ownership, it was time to call for larger and more powerful locomotives.

The LSWR works at Nine Elms had recently introduced a new class of shunter, the B4, designed by William Adams. These were compact, sturdy and powerful 0-4-0Ts with a short wheelbase, and were found to be ideally suited to the tight curves and restricted quayside conditions at Southampton. Thus, in November 1893, two of the class were dispatched to the docks. These were Nos 81 and 176, which became *Jersey* and *Guernsey* on transfer to the Docks Department, being quickly followed by 96 and 97 as *Normandy* and *Brittany* in the following month.

The main dimensions of the B4 class were:

Cylinders:	16in x 22in
Driving wheels:	3ft 9¾in
Wheelbase:	7ft 0in
Working pressure:	140psi
Tank capacity:	600gal
Weight:	33ton 9cwt

Another quartet of B4s had arrived at the docks by spring 1896 - Nos 86, 93, 95, and 102, bearing the names of *Havre*, *St Malo*, *Honfleur* and *Granville*. Then, Nos 85 and 98 (*Alderney* and *Cherbourg* respectively) followed in April and May 1900.

B4s Nos 89 and 90, as *Trouville* and *Caen*, were transferred to the docks in March 1901. Their arrival signalled the demise of *Canute,* which was relegated to the lowly status of a stationary boiler, while *Ascupart* and *Sir Bevis* were only steamed occasionally. *Vulcan* and *Ironside* were transferred to duties at Bournemouth shed and Poole Quay, while *Bretwalda* and *Clausentum* were sent to take over the Royal Pier duties from the departing Shanks' locos (see Chapter 8).

A bevy of B4s assembled at the Docks Locomotive Shed in 1903. (Southampton University Industrial Archaeology Group)

The compliment of B4s in the docks in June 1903 remained at twelve, and in the same year, the three remaining Dock Company engines left the scene. *Sir Bevis* was purchased by C.D. Philips of Newport, South Wales in March, while October saw *Ascupart* sold, and last recorded at sea on a journey to Australia. In the same month, *Canute* was sold for scrap and broken up at the docks. Thus, the replacement of the old regime was complete.

By April 1908, Nos 746 and 747 (similar to the B4, but officially class K14) carrying the names *Dinan* and *Dinard* had arrived and, following their appearance, the old two-road running shed was rebuilt to accommodate the growing fleet now numbering fourteen. This became the regular contingent of locos allocated to the Eastern Docks for many decades until rail traffic was virtually ended in the 1970s.

Under the LSWR, the development of the docks continued unabated, and the White Star Line transferred its transatlantic vessels from Liverpool to Southampton in 1907, necessitating yet another expansion of the quayside facilities. The White Star Dock (since renamed the Ocean Dock) was duly completed by 1911, and covering an area of 15.5 acres, was largest of all the open docks. It was also the last major work undertaken in the Eastern Docks with berths numbered 43 to 47, offering almost 4000 feet of quaysides. The remaining berths 48 to 51 were additions adjacent to No 6 dry dock.

Southampton Docks had been known as a premier trooping port since its time as a chief embarkation point for troops destined for the Crimean War from 1854-56. During the Great War of 1914-18, it was again the focal point for supplies of men and machines to the battlefronts of Europe, when some 8,000,000 men, 850,000 horses, 3,500,000 tons of stores and 180,000 vehicles passed through its gates.

The B4s were occasionally supplemented by the odd C14 class locomotives, that were otherwise employed at the terminus yard or the Town Quay (see Chapter 7), but they adequately handled the ensuing duties until the grouping of the railway companies saw the Southern Railway assume control of the docks in 1923. However, one operational problem that did occur in the 1920s was the amount of scaling in the boilers due to the quality of the docks water supply. To counteract this, the locos were fitted with linseed oil filters to remove impurities, but the practice ceased during World War II due to a shortage of linseed, and the filters were removed.

This view from the roof of the South Western Hotel shows a busy docks scene in the early 1900s. The LSWR Invoicing Office in the bottom right of the picture was once the residence of the Docks Engineer and is one of the few original buildings remaining in the Eastern Docks. Immediately behind it is an area that became the Engineer's Department Yard. (Author's Collection)

LSWR B4 Class 0-4-0T No 81 *Jersey*

Name:	*Jersey*
Manufacturer:	LSWR at Nine Elms Works
Built:	1893
Running number:	81 (LSWR)
At the docks:	1893-1947

Jersey arrived new at Southampton Docks from Nine Elms in November 1893 (accompanied by sister engine *Guernsey*) as the first of the class to replace the former Dock Company locos. After many years of stalwart service, it left the docks in 1947 when the B4s were displaced by the USA class tanks; it was then based at Eastleigh on general duties. Still retaining its name, it was sold by BR in April 1949 to D. Zeiler & Co who were agents for Stewarts and Lloyds. However, *Jersey* was then resold to the Doncaster firm of Bell, who in September of that year, passed it on to the Skinningrove Iron Company Ltd near Saltburn. There it had a new lease of life for some twelve years, working on until it was scrapped in June 1961.

B4 Class "Jersey" in its days at the docks. (Bert Moody Collection)

LSWR B4 Class 0-4-0T No 85 *Alderney*

Name:	*Alderney*
Manufacturer:	LSWR at Nine Elms Works
Built:	1891
Running number:	85 (LSWR)
At the docks:	1900–1947

Built in October 1891, No 85 saw service at Plymouth before arriving at the docks in April 1900 as *Alderney* where it worked with others of the class until replaced by the USA tanks in 1947. *Alderney* saw little service after leaving its maritime career, and after a period of storage at Eastleigh, it was finally withdrawn from general service in January 1949 and scrapped.

See page 11 for an illustration of this locomotive.

LSWR B4 Class 0-4-0T No 86 *Havre*

Name:	*Havre*
Manufacturer:	LSWR at Nine Elms Works
Built:	1891
Running number:	86 (LSWR) 30086 (BR)
At the docks:	1896-1947

Following duties at Plymouth No 86 arrived at Southampton Docks as *Havre* in February 1896, where it worked until being displaced by the USA class tanks. *Havre* was transferred to Stewarts Lane depot in April 1947, and became the first of the class to be given a BR number (30086) at Ashford Works in September 1948. This it carried until finally withdrawn from service in March 1959 and scrapped.

LSWR B4 Class 0-4-0T No 89 *Trouville*

Name:	*Trouville*
Manufacturer:	LSWR at Nine Elms Works
Built:	1892
Running number:	89 (LSWR) 30089 (BR)
At the docks:	1901-1947

No 89 was built in November 1892, and after working at Salisbury and Bournemouth, arrived at Southampton Docks as *Trouville* in March 1901, where it joined others of the class, working there until displaced by the USA class tanks. On leaving the docks, it was transferred to Brighton depot in April 1947, and worked at Kingston Wharf, Shoreham. After further duties at Plymouth during the 1950s, running as BR No 30089 it became shed pilot at Guildford in 1961, and was subsequently replaced by a USA tank for the second time in March 1963, whereupon it was withdrawn from service and scrapped.

LSWR B4 Class 0-4-0T No 90 *Caen*

Name:	*Caen*
Manufacturer:	LSWR at Nine Elms Works
Built:	1892
Running number:	90 (LSWR)
At the docks:	1901-1947

No 90 was built in November 1892, and employed at Northam, where it spent much of its time shuttling back and forth to Southampton Docks. It then made a permanent move to the docks as *Caen* in March 1901, where it worked until displaced by the USA tanks. On leaving the docks, *Caen* was briefly employed at Stewarts Lane depot before becoming the first of the class to be withdrawn from service in May 1948 prior to being scrapped at Eastleigh.

LSWR B4 Class 0-4-0T No 93 *St Malo*

Name:	*St Malo*
Manufacturer:	LSWR at Nine Elms Works
Built:	1892
Running number:	93 (LSWR) 30093 (BR)
At the docks:	1896 - 1947

No 93 was built in December 1892, and after spending its early years shunting at Nine Elms, arrived at Southampton Docks in April 1896 as *St Malo*, following a spell of duty at Northam. Thereafter, it remained with others of the class until being displaced. On leaving the docks, it was transferred to Bournemouth, and was usually stationed there until broken up after withdrawal in April 1960.

LSWR B4 Class 0-4-0T No 95 *Honfleur*

Name:	*Honfleur*
Manufacturer:	LSWR at Nine Elms Works
Built:	1893
Running number:	95 (LSWR)
At the docks:	1896–1947

No 95 was built in April 1893, and performed initial duties shunting at Nine Elms Works before arriving at Southampton Docks as *Honfleur* in February 1896. Like its fellow B4s, it was displaced by the USA tanks, and was afterwards sold by BR to the Ministry of Fuel & Power in spring 1949, with whom it worked at several opencast mining sites including Wernos, Ammanford in Carmarthenshire, and Gwaun-cse-Gurwen in Glamorganshire, until being scrapped in October 1957.

See page 11 for an illustration of this locomotive.

"Trouville", pictured at an unknown location, possibly at Plymouth. (Bert Moody Collection)

B4 Class "Caen" at the Eastern Docks in September 1931. (O.J. Morris)

B4 Class "St Malo" in the Eastern Docks near Canute Road. (Author's Collection)

LSWR B4 Class 0-4-0T No 96 *Normandy*

Name:	*Normandy*
Manufacturer:	LSWR at Nine Elms Works
Built:	1893
Running number:	96 (LSWR) 30096 (BR)
At the docks:	1893–1947

Normandy (along with sister *Brittany*) arrived new at Southampton Docks in December 1893, being the second delivery from Nine Elms Works in their systematic replacement of the old Dock Company locos. After their careers in the docks, many of the class were dispersed around the SR region after overhaul at Eastleigh, but *Normandy* was retained there for a while, eventually moving on to Winchester before being taken out of BR service in October 1963.

Many others of the class had already been sold off to industrial sites around the country, and in February 1964, *Normandy* joined their ranks when purchased by Corralls Ltd at Dibles Wharf in Southampton (see Chapter 14). There, the new owners renamed the loco *Corrall Queen*, but during its years at Northam it retained its former BR number on the smokebox door until December 1972 saw it pass to the Bulleid Preservation Society. Now, once again sporting its original name *Normandy*, the veteran enjoys an active retirement on the Bluebell Railway.

LSWR B4 Class 0-4-0T No 97 *Brittany*

Name:	*Brittany*
Manufacturer:	LSWR at Nine Elms Works
Built:	1893
Running number:	97 (LSWR)
At the docks:	1893–1947

Brittany arrived new at Southampton Docks together with *Normandy* in December 1893 as part of the programme to replace the former Dock Company locos. After withdrawal from the docks, *Brittany* was taken into storage at Eastleigh, until being withdrawn from service in February 1949. In September of that year, it became one of a number of the class sold to D. Zeiler & Co, acting on behalf of Stewarts & Lloyds who employed the loco at their Bilston works in Staffordshire, where it rejoined forces with *Cherbourg* and *Guernsey*. Retaining its name until the end, *Brittany* continued working until being taken out of service in June 1958, and was scrapped soon afterwards.

LSWR B4 Class 0-4-0T No 98 *Cherbourg*

Name:	*Cherbourg*
Manufacturer:	LSWR at Nine Elms Works
Built:	1893
Running number:	98 (LSWR)
At the docks:	1900-1947

As with others of the class, No 98 began its working life shunting at Nine Elms before its arrival at Southampton Docks as *Cherbourg* in May 1900. There, it worked until the B4s were replaced in 1947, following which it was transferred to Eastleigh, and sold to Stewarts & Lloyds Ltd at Bilston in February 1949 where it was reunited with *Brittany* and *Guernsey* later that year. It remained there until being broken up in 1958, retaining its name until the end.

B4 Class "Normandy" pictured at Eastleigh on 2nd October 1948. (S.C. Nash)

"Brittany" at work near the Eastern Docks Engineer's Yard on 4th September 1937. (S.W. Baker)

"Cherbourg" rests awhile near the Eastern Docks running shed. (Bert Moody Collection)

LSWR B4 Class 0-4-0T No 102 *Granville*

Name:	*Granville*
Manufacturer:	LSWR at Nine Elms Works
Built:	1893
Running number:	102 (LSWR) 30102 (BR)
At the docks:	1896–1947 and 1961

After its initial years shunting at Nine Elms Works, No 102, having been built in April 1893, arrived at Southampton Docks in April 1896 named *Granville*. Here, it worked until replaced by a USA tank. *Granville* was then transferred to Eastleigh, after which followed spells at Poole Quay and Winchester, before a brief return to the docks in July 1961.

Withdrawal came in September 1963, but in June the following year it was saved from the scrapheap when purchased by Butlins, and placed on static display at their holiday camp at Skegness. In March 1971, *Granville* was moved to its present location at the Bressingham Steam Museum in Norfolk where, after some restoration, it remains on public view, being one of only two survivors of the class, the other being No 96 *Normandy* on the Bluebell Line.

LSWR B4 Class 0-4-0T No 176 *Guernsey*

Name:	*Guernsey*
Manufacturer:	LSWR at Nine Elms Works
Built:	1893
Running number:	176 (LSWR)
At the docks:	1893-1947

Guernsey arrived new at Southampton Docks in November 1893, along with sister engine *Jersey* as the first wave of replacements for the ageing former Dock Company stock. Like the other B4s, it worked in the docks until 1947.

After becoming surplus to BR requirements in June 1948, *Guernsey* and several others of the class were sold to D. Zeigler and Co, on behalf of Stewarts & Lloyds during the following year. In September 1949, it was dispatched by them (along with sister engine *Brittany*) to rejoin *Cherbourg* at Bilston, Staffordshire. There, whilst retaining its original name, it saw another decade of activity, and apart from a brief loan spell to the Stanton Ironworks Company Ltd, Nottingham, (between December 1955 and March 1956), *Guernsey* remained in service until being declared redundant in 1959 and was finally broken up in February 1961.

LSWR K14 Class 0-4-0T No 746 *Dinan*

Name:	*Dinan*
Manufacturer:	LSWR at Nine Elms Works
Built:	1908
Running number:	746 (LSWR) 101 (LSWR)
At the docks:	1908-1947

Five K14 class locos were built in 1908 as Dugald Drummond's version of the original B4 engines designed by William Adams, although the new engines were still commonly regarded as B4s. No 746 was one of two supplied new to Southampton Docks as *Dinan* (the other being *Dinard*) in April that year to compliment the dozen B4s already stationed there.

In February 1922, *Dinan* was renumbered to 101 due to stock reorganisation, and continued as such in the docks until the arrival of the USA tanks. Little "outside" work was found and *Dinan* was consequently withdrawn from service in November 1948. However, in October the following year, was sold for £750 to Taylor Woodrow & Co for work on the construction of the East Yelland power station near Barnstable as their No SL2. There it remained until the middle of 1952 when the owners returned the loco to their Southall premises, and it was finally disposed of in 1954.

B4 Class "Granville" pictured near the Docks shed in 1937. (RCTS)

Early days for B4 Class "Guernsey" at Nine Elms. (Author's Collection)

K14 class No 746 "Dinan" in early days at Nine Elms. (R.K. Blencowe Collection)

LSWR K14 Class 0-4-0T No 747 *Dinard*

Name:	*Dinard*
Manufacturer:	LSWR at Nine Elms Works
Built:	1908
Running number:	747 (LSWR) 147 (LSWR)
At the docks:	1908 - 1947

No 747 was the second K14 class locomotive to be delivered new to Southampton Docks in April 1908. Carrying the name *Dinard*, it partnered its sister engine *Dinan* and the fleet of twelve B4s already established there.

In February 1922, *Dinard* was renumbered 147 due to stock reorganisation and continued working in the docks until 1947. *Dinard* was then transferred to Nine Elms for shed pilot duties until being withdrawn from BR service in February 1949. Like its sister *Dinan* it was purchased by Taylor Woodrow & Co for £750 and, as their No SL1, was sent to work at an open cast site at Waun Wen, near Blaenavon before moving on to the Blaenavon Company Ltd in the latter part of 1951. There it carried the name *Blaenavon* until being scrapped in late 1958.

"Dinard" at the docks in July 1938. (F.A. Wycherley / R.S. Carpenter Collection)

CHAPTER 3

Southern Railway Docks 1923-1947

At the grouping on 1st January 1923, the formation of the Southern Railway saw the amalgamation of the vast locomotive stocks accumulated by the former independent railways. Where there were duplicate numbers, they were preceded by a prefix letter of "E" (LSWR, Eastleigh), "B" (LBSCR, Brighton) and "A" (SECR, Ashford). This system prevailed until a comprehensive renumbering in 1931, when 1000 was added to SECR locos, and 2000 to those of the LBSCR. From the early days of the SR, numerous engines found themselves transferred to "foreign" climes and the docks was no exception.

As with previous administrations, the Southern Railway had plans to expand the docks, and in 1927 work commenced to build a huge new extension along the River Test from the old West Quay to Millbrook. Berths 101 to 109 were created in a continuous quay some 7500ft long. The scheme culminated at its western end with the construction of the King George V Graving Dock (later No 7 dry dock) and the whole works were finally completed in 1935.

In 1899, the former LSWR Chief Mechanical Engineer, Dugald Drummond had an unusual combination of locomotive and saloon built as his personal transport to enable him to travel to work from his home at Surbiton to Nine Elms, and to tour his domain in relative comfort. Known unflatteringly as *The Bug*, it fell out of use after his demise in 1912, but during the latter stages of the docks works, it found itself pressed into Departmental Service (see Chapter 5) as No 58S. From 1932, VIPs were taken on tours of the vast site aboard this odd looking vehicle, and on busy days when visitor numbers required it, a six wheeled trailing coach was attached.

The "New Docks", as they were initially called, also reclaimed over 400 acres of marsh and mudflats between the quaysides and the former Western Shore, and here was built a large industrial estate with three massive marshalling yards. This effectively doubled the amount of track, and increased the rail network throughout the port to some 78 miles in total.

The great expanse of berths and yards heaped more pressure on the shunting resources, which required long hours of round-the-clock working, with engines spending over a third of their time working continuously 24 hours per day. As a result, fresh crews were frequently called upon – sometimes from Eastleigh or Fratton when numbers were short. In summer 1936, meetings were held to discuss increasing the docks locomotive staff by six, instead of constantly calling on outsiders, and it was agreed to engage this extra number – but only from June to September. At that time, drivers were paid 12s (60p) to 16s (80p) per eight-hour shift, and firemen from 9s 6d (47½p) to 12s (60p).

With the docks now effectively twice its original size, other locos were required to augment the resident B4s, not only as replacements for those under repair, but as additional routine motive power. Many visits were "one offs", with Eastleigh-based shunters being brought in at short notice, but a number of tanks were drafted in on an almost permanent basis. In particular, some ex-Brighton D1 class locomotives (Nos 240, 633 and 359) were transferred from Exmouth Junction to the docks by 1934.

The docks shed on 8th March 1936 was still mainly inhabited by B4s. (H.N. James)

It was considered they would serve a more useful purpose here on general duties and carriage heating, but by the outbreak of World War II, all had been moved to other locations. Previously, all had carried names, but all had been removed when new liveries were applied in May 1905.

The main dimensions of the D1 class were:

Cylinders: 17in x 24in
Driving wheels: 5ft 6in
Wheelbase: 7ft 7in
Working pressure: 170psi
Tank capacity: 860gal
Weight: 43ton 10cwt

At the centre of the New Docks, a carriage cleaning and warming shed was constructed, that could accommodate six made-up passenger boat trains. Four docks locomotives became permanently allocated there for steam heating, together with general duties in the adjacent yards; the shed also had facilities for the loco crews and shunting staff. To the immediate west of the carriage shed, a new Engineer's Department yard was laid out, and this housed a resident loco for several years (see Chapter 5).

During the war years of 1939-45, Southampton again played its part as a front line port when, once again, unprecedented totals of men and equipment passed over its quaysides. The dry docks were continuously employed in repairs to hospital ships, troop carriers, merchant vessels and fleet auxiliaries, while heavy air raids were especially prevalent during 1940-41. Despite all this, the docks freight traffic continued at intense levels with the handling of supplies from America, and Commonwealth countries for distribution around the nation. All this culminated in the D-day invasion, when Southampton was one of the prime embarkation points for troop trains and unimaginable volumes of military equipment.

The Brighton E1 class locos once totalled 79, and having been designed by William Stroudley, they were built between 1874 and 1891. By the latter end of the war years, several of the class had made their way to the docks, notably Nos 2112, 2156, 2162 and 2689, which were drafted there in Summer 1943, some remaining until the early 1950s. Like the D1s, all had carried names before the new livery was applied in May 1905.

The main dimensions of the E1 class were as follows:

Cylinders: 17in x 24in
Driving wheels: 4ft 6in
Wheelbase: 7ft 6in
Working pressure: 140psi
Tank capacity: 900gal
Weight: 39ton 10cwt

The new Carriage Shed in the Western Docks became home base to four locomotives. This view, taken on its completion on 2nd January 1936, shows the inaugural train headed by an unidentified B4. (Associated British Ports)

SOUTHERN RAILWAY DOCKS 1923-1947

By 1945, many of the B4s had been at work for almost half a century, and were beginning to show their age with burst boiler tubes and firebox repairs commonplace. So, when hostilities finally ceased, the Southern Railway began to look for replacements. The Docks shed loco allocation in December 1945 was 81/5/6/9/90/3/5-8, 101/2/47/76, 2112/56/62, and 2689.

At that time, a large number of War Department locos were surplus to requirements, including several ex-US Army Transportation Corps 0-6-0Ts dumped at Newbury Racecourse. In May 1946, War Department No 4326 (later numbered 74 by the SR) began a series of comprehensive trials around the docks, and having proved successful over several months, the class was accepted as successors to the B4s. As many of the "Yanks" had hardly been used, the cost of £2,500 apiece was very agreeable, and before the end of the year thirteen more (plus a spare) had been towed to Eastleigh for modifications, prior to onward transit to the docks during the following year.

The first of these to arrive were Nos 70 and 72 in April 1947, while Nos 62, 66 and 67 (plus the newly customized No 74) all appeared the following month. Nos 64 and 73 came in June, and Nos 63 and 68 turned up in October. The remainder, comprising Nos 61, 65, 69 and 71, were all there by November.

The main dimensions of the USA tanks were:

Cylinders: 16½ in x 24in
Driving wheels: 4ft 6in
Wheelbase: 10ft 0in
Working pressure: 210psi
Tank capacity: 1000gal
Weight: 46ton 10cwt

As each batch arrived, the B4s were dispersed to other locations until finally being sold out of service or broken up. However, several of the old stalwarts returned to the fold in later years when extra locos were demanded due to volume of work, repairs or maintenance. These visits also included others of the class that had not previously been stationed there.

After leaving the docks, some of the class were stationed at Eastleigh while others travelled further afield, and their names were systematically removed upon being repainted. *Trouville* went to Brighton, *Havre* and *Caen* went to Stewarts Lane, while *Dinard* went to Nine Elms and *St Malo* to Bournemouth. *Caen* was the first to be scrapped in May 1948, followed by *Alderney* in January 1949.

Jersey, *Guernsey*, *Cherbourg*, *Brittany*, *Honfleur*, *Dinan*, *Dinard*, *Normandy* and *Granville* were all eventually sold to new owners, the last two surviving into preservation.

The "new order" was in place, but big changes were in the offing as Nationalisation loomed on the horizon. On 1st January 1948, the docks and its railways passed into public ownership.

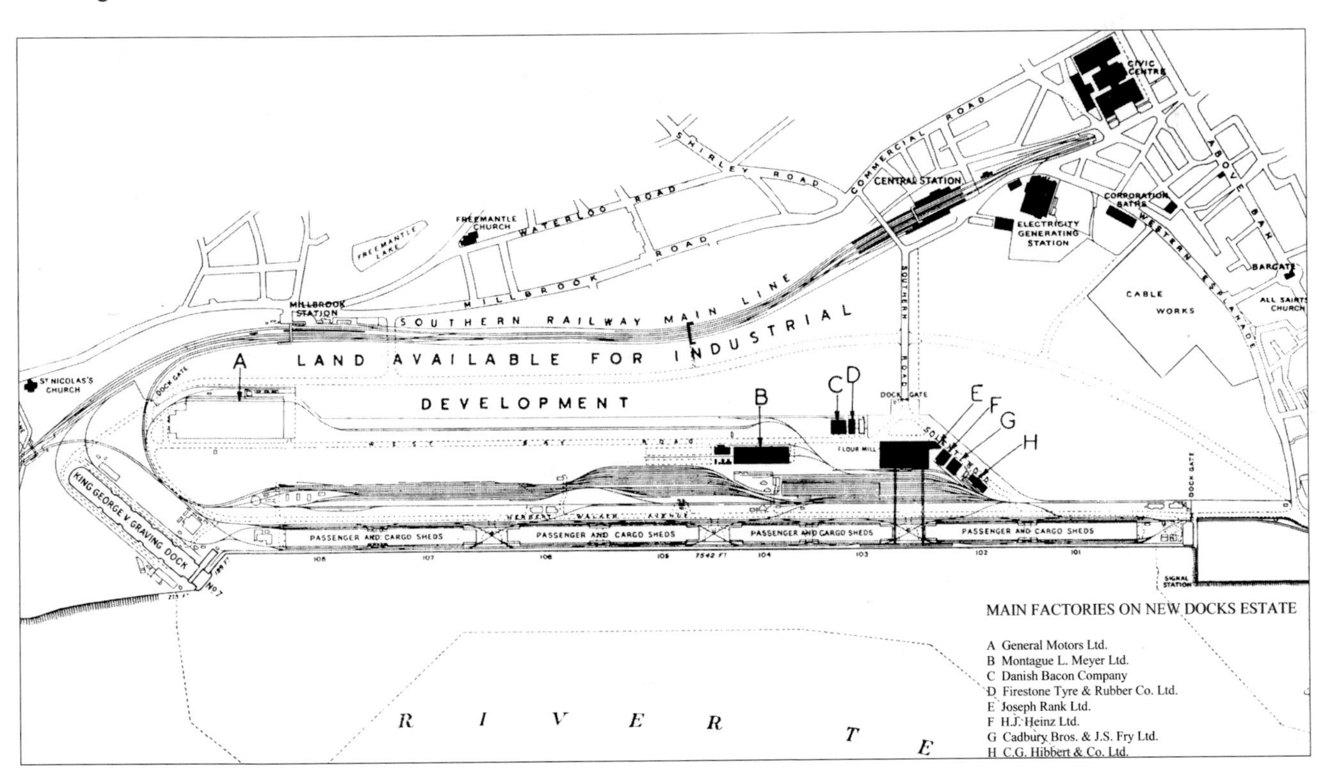

Plan of the New Docks, completed in 1935.

LBSCR Class D1 0-4-2T No 240

Name:	(*Ditchling*)
Manufacturer:	Neilson & Co, Glasgow
Built:	1881
Works number:	2709
Running number:	240 (LBSCR) 2240 (SR)
At the docks:	1933-1937

Although the D1 class designed by William Stroudley totalled 125, some 35 of the engines were built by Neilson & Co of Glasgow because Brighton Works was already at full capacity. No 240, originally named *Ditchling*, was supplied by Neilsons in November 1881 for London suburban and main line passenger train working, and was based at New Cross shed. In December 1922, as No 240, it was stationed at Midhurst. In Southern Railway days it was renumbered 2240 in 1931, and located at Exmouth Junction, from where it arrived at the Docks via Eastleigh in September 1933, remaining there until at least 1937.

During World War II, the LMS was short of engines, but 2240 was deemed surplus to SR requirements, and in August 1941, it was transferred to work in the Liverpool area (along with 2286). Then, in May 1942, the two were acquired by the War Department, and saw duty on the Melbourne and Longmoor Military Railways. After the war ended, 2240 was loaned to Moira Collieries, Leicestershire, for several months before being stored at Horsham, and finally scrapped August 1946.

LBSCR Class D1 0-4-2T No 286

Name:	(*Ranmore*)
Manufacturer:	LBSCR, Brighton Works
Built:	1879
Running number:	286 (LBSCR), 2286 (SR)
At the docks:	1934–1937

Another of the class of 125 locomotives designed by William Stroudley for London suburban working and some main line duties, No 286 was built in July 1879 and named *Ranmore*. It was initially stationed at New Cross shed, but in December 1922, it was stationed at Brighton, and then overhauled at Newhaven in January 1932. By November 1934, as No 2286, it had made its first appearance at Southampton Docks, where it became a regular until at least October 1937. With No 2240, it was loaned to the LMS in August 1941, for whom the pair worked together in the Liverpool area. They then moved to the War Department in May 1942, and were employed on the Melbourne and Longmoor Military Railways. When the war ended, 2286 was stored at Nine Elms and eventually scrapped in July 1948.

LBSCR Class D1 0-4-2T No 33

Name:	(*Mitcham*)
Manufacturer:	LBSCR, Brighton Works
Built:	1876
Running number:	33, 633 (both LBSCR), B633 (SR)
At the docks:	1934-1936

No 33 (named *Mitcham*) was built in May 1876, and allocated to New Cross shed, being renumbered 633 in December 1908. Modifications were made prior to its transfer to Exmouth Junction in April 1929, where restrictions to the coal and water capacities allowed it to run on the weight-restricted Axminster to Lyme Regis branch. B633 eventually arrived at the docks as one of a trio of D1s from Exmouth Junction in September 1934, and its spell at Southampton ended in March 1936, when it was transferred to Bognor Regis. By October 1937, it was back at Exmouth Junction being used as a stationary boiler, and it remained so until it was scrapped in February 1944. Having spent its final years in a dilapidated state, it earned the distinction of being the last Brighton loco to carry a "B" prefix to its number.

LBSCR Class D1 0-4-2T No 359

Name:	(*Egmont*)
Manufacturer:	LBSCR, Brighton Works
Built:	1886
Running number:	359 (LBSCR), 2359 (SR)
At the docks:	1934-1937

Built in December 1886 as No 359, and named *Egmont*, this locomotive was initially stationed at New Cross for work on London suburban lines and occasional main line services, and by December 1922, it was still at New Cross.

In September 1929, this loco was modified at Brighton works for use on the weight-restricted Axminster to Lyme Regis branch. As with No 633 some months earlier, limitations were imposed on its coal and water capacities, and the loco was dispatched to Exmouth Junction where it was later overhauled in March 1930. From there it came to Southampton in September 1934. In June 1936, while in the docks, the loco sustained slight frame damage in a freak accident. While the engine was stationary, a brake van (No 326) was blown by a gust of wind, and a collision occurred, causing minor damage to the loco frames. 2359 was still at the docks in October 1937, but by April 1941, was at Eastleigh. Here, it was intended to be fitted with fire-fighting equipment, but instead, it was converted to a mobile washing plant, and by August 1942, it had been dispatched to its original haunt at New Cross.

At the end of the war, it was in use as a stationary boiler at Redhill, and from there it was taken to Dover, where it served the same purpose from January 1947. At Nationalisation, it was allocated the number 32359, but never carried it before being scrapped in July 1951 as the last BR example of its class.

LBSCR No 359 "Egmont" still carries its name in pre-1905 livery. (D. Searle Collection)

Southern Railway USA Class 0-6-0T No 61

Manufacturer:	H.K. Porter, Pittsburgh, USA
Built:	1942
Works number:	7420
Running number:	1264 (US Army), 61 (SR) 30061, DS233 (both BR)
At the docks:	1947-1962

Built in 1942 (by Porter as works No 7420), WD 1264 arrived at Eastleigh in late 1946 from the War Department dump at Newbury Racecourse. After modification, it was dispatched to work in the docks in November of the following year, as Southern Railway No 61. As this was the only Porter-built loco purchased (the others were all by Vulcan) a second engine (WD 1261) was acquired for spares and kept at Eastleigh. Many parts were transferred in refits during its time at the docks.

At Nationalisation, No 61 became No 30061, and September 1955 saw it go on loan to the London Midland Region (along with 30066) where it was based at Kentish Town. However, it returned to the docks in October that year, until another spell with LMS saw it working at Cricklewood from September 1956 until January 1957. Back at the docks, it remained working until the class was replaced by a fleet of diesels in 1962. By September that year, it had been condemned at Eastleigh but it avoided the scrap heap by being transferred to Departmental Stock as No DS233; it was sent to Redbridge Sleeper Depot a month later. There it remained, although occasionally it was recalled for dock service, until once again being replaced by a diesel in March 1967. This time there was no reprieve, and 30061 was scrapped soon afterwards.

Southern Railway USA Class 0-6-0T No 62

Manufacturer:	Vulcan Iron Works, Wilkes-Barre, USA
Built:	1942
Works number:	4375
Running number:	1277 (US Army), 62 (SR), 30062, DS234 (both BR)
At the docks:	1947-1962

This loco arrived at Eastleigh as WD 1277, and commenced work at the docks in May 1947 as Southern Railway No 62, becoming BR No 30062 at Nationalisation in 1948. It remained at the docks until the class was replaced by diesels in May 1962, after which it was transferred to Departmental Stock as No DS234, and sent to Meldon Quarry at Okehampton in December that year. By August 1966, repairs were needed, and it was taken out of service, being replaced for a short time by No 30064. DS234 was finally broken up in March 1967.

Southern Railway USA Class 0-6-0T No 63

Manufacturer:	Vulcan Iron Works, Wilkes-Barre, USA
Built:	1942
Works number:	4382
Running number:	1284 (US Army), 63 (SR) 30063 (BR)
At the docks:	1947-1962

This Vulcan-built locomotive arrived at Eastleigh as WD 1284, before transfer to the docks as Southern Railway No 63 in October 1947. It became No 30063 at Nationalisation in 1948, and remained in the docks until replaced by a diesel in May 1962. Unlike others of the class that went on to work in different locations, 30063 had suffered damage in a collision, and was immediately condemned and scrapped in June 1962.

Former Docks USA No 30061 returns from Redbridge to its old haunts as DS233 in June 1964. (TLP Collection)

USA No 30062 at the Docks in May 1953. (Bert Moody Collection)

USA No 63 at the New Docks in April 1950, with a further three other unidentified USA tanks. (Millbrook House / R.S. Carpenter Collection)

Southern Railway USA Class 0-6-0T No 64

Manufacturer:	Vulcan Iron Works, Wilkes-Barre, USA
Built:	1942
Works number:	4432
Running number:	1959 (US Army), 64 (SR), 30064 (BR)
At the docks:	1947-1962

WD 1959 arrived at the docks in June 1947, where it saw unbroken service until May 1962. It was then based at Eastleigh until, in August 1966, it was dispatched to replace DS234 (ex-30062) at Meldon Quarry, but its visit was short as by October that year it had been replaced by a diesel once again. However, during its short stay it did achieve the distinction of being the last steam locomotive to work on the Western Region before returning to general duties at Eastleigh. When steam traction came to an end in July 1967, No 30064 was stored at Salisbury, along with 30067, 30069, 30071 and 30072, all awaiting their fate. In December that year, it was purchased by the Southern Preservation Company Ltd, and arrived at Liss in Hants, before finding a new home on the Bluebell Railway, arriving there in October 1971.

Southern Railway USA Class 0-6-0T No 65

Manufacturer:	Vulcan Iron Works, Wilkes-Barre, USA
Built:	1943
Works number:	4441
Running number:	1968 (US Army), 65 (SR), 30065, DS237 (both BR), 22 (K&ESR)
At the docks:	1947-1962

In common with the others, WD 1968 arrived at Eastleigh in 1946, before transferring to the docks as Southern Railway No 65 in November 1947, where it worked until May 1962. By November 1963, it had been transferred to Departmental Stock as No DS237 and named *Maunsell* (after the SR Chief Mechanical Engineer) for duties at Ashford Works, where it joined former docks stable-mate DS238 (ex-30070 now named *Wainwright*).

It remained at Ashford until taken out of service in April 1967, after which it was sold as scrap to Woodhams Bros at Barry Island, together with DS238. During the run to Wales, they developed mechanical problems and were stored at Tonbridge awaiting repair until being abandoned by Woodhams, and sold off to the Kent and East Sussex Railway in August 1968. At the Rolvenden workshops of the K&ESR, this loco was given the number 22 (*Wainwright* becoming No 21) and the pair still enjoy an active retirement there.

Southern Railway USA Class 0-6-0T No 66

Manufacturer:	Vulcan Iron Works, Wilkes-Barre, USA
Built:	1942
Works number:	4377
Running number:	1279 (US Army), 66 (SR), 30066, DS235 (both BR)
At the docks:	1947-1962

Originally WD 1279, this locomotive became SR No 66, and carried out its duties in the docks until loaned (together with No 30061) to the London Midland Region in September 1955, where it was transferred to Bank Hall, Liverpool for a few weeks, both locomotives returning to Southampton in October that year. No 65 remained at the docks until the class was withdrawn in May 1962.

By March 1963, it had been transferred to Departmental Stock as No DS235, firstly being sent to Ashford Works, and then being hired to Betteshanger Colliery, Kent, before arriving at Lancing Carriage Works in June of that year. There it teamed up again with former docks running-mate DS236 (ex-30074). When the works closed in June 1965, the pair went back to Eastleigh, where they were scrapped in August the same year.

USAs No 30064 and No 30073 in tandem alongside the Docks Ocean Terminal. (Bert Moody Collection)

USA No 30065 on Eastern Docks duty. (Author's Collection)

USA No 30066 near Drydock No 3 on 11th June 1949. (R.K. Blencowe Collection)

Southern Railway USA Class 0-6-0T No 67

Manufacturer:	Vulcan Iron Works, Wilkes-Barre, USA
Built:	1942
Works number:	4380
Running number:	1282 (US Army), 67 (SR), 30067 (BR)
At the docks:	1947-1962

Built in 1942 as War Department No 1282, this locomotive became SR No 67, arriving at Southampton in May 1947, where it remained in service until being replaced by a diesel in May 1962. After a spell of general duties, the end of steam came to the Southern Region in June 1967, and as BR No 30067, it was taken out of service and stored at Salisbury, together with sister engines 30064, 30069, 30071 and 30072, awaiting its fate. The end came when it was broken up a month later.

Southern Railway USA Class 0-6-0T No 68

Manufacturer:	Vulcan Iron Works, Wilkes-Barre, USA
Built:	1943
Works number:	4444
Running number:	1971 (US Army), 68 (SR), 30068 (BR
At the docks:	1947-1962

Built in 1943, WD 1971 was sent to work in the docks from October 1947 as SR No 68. Withdrawn in May 1962, this loco, by now BR No 30068, was considered for transfer to Departmental Stock, but was found to be in such poor mechanical condition that it was overlooked in favour of No 30074. It was eventually taken out of service and broken up in April 1964.

Southern Railway USA Class 0-6-0T No 69

Manufacturer:	Vulcan Iron Works, Wilkes-Barre, USA
Built:	1943
Works number:	4425
Running number:	1952 (US Army), 69 (SR), 30069 (BR)
At the docks:	1947-1962

As WD 1952, this locomotive was overhauled Eastleigh, and sent to Southampton in November 1947. After some fifteen years, it was replaced by a diesel, and as BR No 30069, it was transferred for general duties elsewhere in the region. At the end of steam on the Southern Region in July 1967, it was put into storage at Salisbury depot awaiting disposal, together with Nos 30064, 30067, 30071 and 30072, and was broken up within a few weeks.

USA No 30067 at Southampton Docks Shed in July 1960. (Southern Images)

USA tank No 68 passes 23 berth in SR days at the Eastern Docks. (J.H. Aston)

USA No 30069 at the Docks in August 1951. (F.A. Wycherley / R.S. Carpenter Collection)

Southern Railway USA Class 0-6-0T No 70

Manufacturer:	Vulcan Iron Works, Wilkes-Barre, USA
Built:	1943
Works number:	4433
Running number:	1960 (US Army), 70 (SR), 30070, DS238 (both BR)
At the docks:	1947-1962

Originally War Department No 1960, this locomotive arrived in Southampton in April 1947 after overhaul at Eastleigh. When the class was withdrawn from the docks from May 1962 it was laid up at Eastleigh until the following August saw its transfer to Departmental Stock as No DS238. It was then sent to Ashford Wagon Works, where it was joined by 30065 (DS237) a few months later. As DS238, it was given the name *Wainwright* in honour of the first locomotive superintendent of the SECR, and together with DS237 (as *Maunsell*) it remained there until taken out of service in April 1967.

Two months later *Maunsell* was replaced by a diesel loco and the two USA tanks were sold as scrap to Woodhams Bros at Barry Island, but after developing mechanical problems en route, Woodhams resold them both to the Kent and East Sussex Railway in August 1968. After being transported to Rolvenden, *Wainwright* became No 21 and *Maunsell* was numbered 22. As such they remain in preservation.

Southern Railway USA Class 0-6-0T No 71

Manufacturer:	Vulcan Iron Works, Wilkes-Barre, USA
Built:	1943
Works number:	4444
Running number:	1966 (US Army), 71 (SR), 30071 (BR)
At the docks:	1947-1962

This loco arrived at Southampton as No 71 in November 1947 after an overhaul at Eastleigh, and then remained in the docks until the class was replaced in May 1962. Afterwards, it saw general service in the region until laid aside and stored at Salisbury with Nos 30064, 30067, 30069 and 30072 in July 1967. It was scrapped soon afterwards

Southern Railway USA Class 0-6-0T No 72

Manufacturer:	Vulcan Iron Works, Wilkes-Barre, USA
Built:	1943
Works number:	4446
Running number:	1973 (US Army), 72 (SR), 30072 (BR)
At the docks:	1947-1962

No 72 arrived at the docks in April 1947 after overhaul at Eastleigh, and stayed until May 1962, after which it became shed pilot at Guildford, ironically, taking over from a B4 class loco (No 30089) as it had done previously at the docks. By July 1967, it was in storage at Salisbury awaiting the breakers torch, but was reprieved when purchased for preservation by the Keighley & Worth Valley Railway, where it remains in service to this day.

USA No 70 at the New Docks in April 1950. (Millbrook House / R.S. Carpenter Collection)

USA No 30071 at Eastleigh Shed in August 1964. (A. Swain)

USA No 72 at the docks in September 1947. (H.C. Casserley / Bert Moody Collection)

Southern Railway USA Class 0-6-0T No 73

Manufacturer:	Vulcan Iron Works, Wilkes-Barre, USA
Built:	1943
Works number:	4447
Running number:	1974 (US Army), 73 (SR), 30073 (BR)
At the docks:	1947-1962

As WD 1974, this locomotive was overhauled at Eastleigh, before becoming SR No 73 at the docks. After being replaced by a diesel in May 1962, it moved to general duties at Eastleigh works in November the following year, where it was eventually withdrawn and scrapped in December 1966.

See page 29 for an illustration of this locomotive.

Southern Railway USA Class 0-6-0T No 74

Manufacturer:	Vulcan Iron Works, Wilkes-Barre, USA
Built:	1943
Works number:	4448
Running number:	4326 (US Army), 30074, DS236 (both BR)
At the docks:	1947-1962

US Army Transportation Corps No 4326 was taken to Eastleigh in April 1946 for overhaul prior to being sent for trials in the docks the following month. Being very successful, the decision was made to replace the ageing B4s and assorted tanks already there with further examples. Officially SR No 74, it never carried that number as it retained its military livery until Nationalisation when it became BR No 30074.

After the arrival of diesels in May 1962, it was taken into Departmental Stock as No DS236 in April 1963, and transferred to Lancing Carriage Works, where it was soon joined by former running mate, DS235 (ex-USA No 30066). The closure of the works in June 1965 spelled the end for the pair who made their final journey back to Eastleigh, and were broken up there in August that year.

USA No74 in army livery at the New Docks in 1947. (Author's Collection)

LBSCR Class E1 0-6-0T No 112

Name:	(*Versailles*)
Manufacturer:	LBSCR, Brighton Works
Built:	1877
Running number:	112 (LBSCR), 2112 (SR)
At the docks:	1943-1945

No 112 was completed in April 1877, and carried the name *Versailles* as it took up shunting duties in the New Cross area. During the 1890s, it was at St Leonards, but after an unsuccessful short period was transferred to Brighton where, like others of the class, it lost its name in a repainting scheme from 1905.

Unlike many of its sisters, this loco survived into Southern Railway days, becoming No 2112 at the 1923 grouping. By March 1929, it was back at New Cross, and April 1932 saw a move to Three Bridges. Wartime service brought a transfer to Eastleigh, with a permanent allocation there from the middle of 1943. By the end of that year, it had joined others of the class (2156, 2162 and 2689) in a move to Southampton Docks, but peacetime found it shunting in the Bournemouth area, where it was condemned in 1948, and broken up in December the following year.

LBSCR Class E1 0-6-0T No 156

Name:	(*Munich*)
Manufacturer:	LBSCR, Brighton Works
Built:	1881
Running number:	156 (LBSCR), 2156 (SR)
At the docks:	1943-1951

Built in March 1881, No 156 entered service in the Battersea area, where it carried the name *Munich*. By March 1929, it had been allocated to New Cross, remaining there until at least April 1932. Under the Southern Railway it became No 2156, and was sent to Exmouth Junction in January 1942 to work at Exeter. By the summer of the following year, it had moved to Eastleigh, and in December, it was sent to the port of Southampton along with other E1s Nos 2112, 2162 and 2689. It saw regular service there into Nationalisation, and was still in the docks in April 1950. This was its final location until it was scrapped in May 1951, never having carried its BR number.

LBSCR No 112 still carries its name in pre-1905 livery. (D. Searle Collection)

LBSCR Class E1 0-6-0T No 162

Name:	(*Southwater*)
Manufacturer:	LBSCR, Brighton Works
Built:	1891
Running number:	162 (LBSCR), 2162 (SR)
At the docks:	1943-1949

This was one of six engines built by Robert Billington, being a modified version of Stroudley's original design. Completed in November 1891, No 162 *Southwater* entered service when allocated to New Cross shed, and spent most of its early years there. By March 1929 it was still at New Cross, but a move to Bricklayers Arms had come about by April 1932. In Southern Railway service, it became 2162, and was transferred to Eastleigh for wartime service in the summer of 1943. By December of that year, it had joined others of the class (2112, 2156, and 2689) at Southampton Docks. This loco survived into BR days, but never received its allocated number of 32162 before being scrapped in November 1949.

LBSCR Class E1 0-6-0T No 89

Name:	(*Brest*)
Manufacturer:	LBSCR, Brighton Works
Built:	1883
Running number:	89, 89A, 689 (all LBSCR), 2689 (SR), 32689 (BR)
At the docks:	1943-1950 and 1955-1960

No 89 entered service in April/May 1883, and was originally named *Brest*. Its initial duties were shunting in the Battersea area and occasionally working the odd light passenger train. This locomotive was rebuilt as class E1X with a larger boiler, tanks and bunker in June 1911, while stationed at Brighton. Following this, it was renumbered 89A in October of that year, and then 689 in December 1912. A move to West Croydon followed, and by March 1929, it had been allocated to New Cross.

After being absorbed into Southern Railway stock, many of the class were withdrawn but, as No 3289, it was reconverted back to class E1 at Eastleigh in March 1930. By April 1932, it was allocated once again to Brighton, but the summer of 1943 saw its return to Eastleigh with an allocation to the docks by the end of that year (along with 2112, 2156 and 2162). By April 1950 it had again returned to Brighton, but by July 1955, it was back at Eastleigh, where it was fitted with radio equipment for a final spell of duty in the docks. There it remained in regular service before being scrapped in February 1960.

E1 tank No 162 at New Cross Gate, circa 1932. (H.F. Wheeller / R.S. Carpenter Collection)

CHAPTER 4

British Railways Docks 1948-1979

From the outset of Nationalisation on 1st January 1948, the port was operated by the British Transport Commission, which oversaw all aspects of public transport, encompassing road, rail and docks management, with all internal railway operations being carried out by BR locomotives and staff.

It was soon apparent that extra motive power was required to work the docks traffic, as despite the Southern Railway's introduction of the powerful USA tanks, several had succumbed to the firebox problems and replacements were needed while they were taken off to Eastleigh for repairs.

The successful introduction of a quartet of Brighton E1 tanks (Nos 2112, 2162, 2156 and 2689) during the latter war years, with the last two remaining into BR days, resulted in others of the class being allocated throughout the 1950s. Nos 32113, 32138, 32151, 32606 and 32694 all made appearances to supplement the docks fleet, which had grown from 14 to 18, four engines being permanently stationed in the New (Western) Docks. Then, as the E1s were taken out of service, the end of the decade saw the introduction of the E2 class on docks duties. Their main dimensions were:

Cylinders:	17½in x 26in
Driving wheels:	4ft 6in
Wheelbase:	8ft 0in
Working pressure:	170psi
Tank capacity:	1090gal
Weight:	52ton 15cwt

This was a class of ten locos built between 1913 and 1916, and designed by L.B. Billington for the LBSCR. All members of the class saw service at Southampton Docks, many of them working there until the end of steam on the dock lines. In addition to the E2 class, a few other individuals were pressed in to docks service, notably O2s, E4s and even the odd A1X, but these were casual callers and short-term replacements.

USA tanks were the mainstay of motive power at the Eastern Docks running shed in BR days during the 1950s. (Author's Collection)

Discussions about "dieselising" the docks loco fleet had been held as early as 1937, but the inevitable decision to replace the ageing steamers with a class of purpose-designed diesel shunters was finally made in 1961. The first of them arrived in June 1962, unceremoniously on a Pickfords lorry!

The 1962 Transport Act saw the docks administration pass from the British Transport Commission to the British Transport Docks Board, thus giving the port operations independence from the railway for the first time since the old Dock Company had sold out to the LSWR in 1892.

The era of docks steam had virtually come to an end – but not quite. For generations, one of the major cargoes in the docks was bananas, shipped in from the Caribbean to the specialised handling facilities at 24/5 berth, where whole stems of the fruit were carried by a conveyor system from the ship's hold directly to rail vans waiting inside the shed. To protect the delicate goods on their onward journey they were packed in straw and the vans were steam-heated. For a while, the odd tank loco was retained for this purpose, until changes in packaging and a switch to road transport rendered the service unnecessary.

At the Western Docks carriage shed, steam was still required for heating the passenger trains, but the need for a locomotive was soon overcome with the introduction of specially-built vans with oil-fired boilers.

By 1967, the dock lines had been reduced from 78 to 66 miles, and in the ensuing years, they had been whittled down to a little over 30. On 4th August 1972, BR announced its intention to discontinue freight working in Southampton Docks, and most of the remaining rail system was gradually dismantled.

By 1975 the fourteen docks diesels had been reduced to a mere five, with only four being rostered at any one time. What little remained of the docks traffic was concentrated in the Western Docks, whilst in the Eastern Docks, all but the basic essentials were removed. The 20 sidings that formed the expanse of the Empress Yard were reduced to a mere three, and the Southern Yard alongside No 5 dry dock had disappeared completely. As if to emphasise the finality of it all, the now derelict docks running shed was demolished in the same year.

Old-time banana handling in the 1930s at 24/5 berth transit shed. (Author's Collection)

Occasional freight movements continued between the Eastern and Western Docks, but these ended in October 1979 when the link past the Town Quay was finally closed. This effectively ended the story of the docks railway system, and by the time the port had been privatised in 1983, the new owners Associated British Ports inherited very little of the internal railway system.

What little remained had been covered in concrete or been cut off and isolated in remote areas. The nature of cargo handling had changed in that car ferries and containerisation relied more on road than rails, and in the present day this once mighty rail network has been reduced to little more than a branch line at either end of the port.

At the Eastern Docks, a single line of rails now enters the Canute Gate to serve the Queen Elizabeth II passenger terminal at 38/9 berth, and to provide a railhead where import and export vehicles are marshalled. At the Western Docks, the line from Millbrook through No 12 gate connects to just a few sidings that serve car trains and bulk storage operations. The Mayflower Cruise Terminal at 105/6 berth relinquished its rail connection in 2003.

The desolate docks running shed awaits the bulldozers on 18th July 1975. (Author)

LBSCR Class E1 0-6-0T No 113

Name:	(*Granville, Durdans*)
Manufacturer:	LBSCR, Brighton Works
Built:	1877
Running number:	113 (LBSCR), 2113 (SR), S2133, 32113 (BR)
At the docks:	1955-1958

No 113 was built in May 1877 and left the workshops for its initial duties at Battersea bearing the name *Granville*. This was changed to *Durdans* in December 1883, before its name was lost altogether in the 1905 repainting scheme. By March 1929, as No 2113, it had been transferred to Croydon, and by April 1932 it had moved to Bricklayers Arms. Then it was on to Tonbridge in May 1938, where it worked until it was placed in storage at Penshurst in May 1940 as a precaution against air raids. In October of the next year, it was back working at Tonbridge, where it saw wartime service shunting military traffic, but by early 1943 it had moved to Reading for a short period before being allocated to Eastleigh.

After the war, Nationalisation saw the renumbering of Southern Region locos into the 3xxxx series, but from February 1948 No 2113 carried a temporary "S" prefix for a while before the new number was applied. In July 1955, this loco was fitted with radio equipment and was sent to work in Southampton Docks, where it worked regularly until being withdrawn from service September 1958.

LBSCR Class E1 0-6-0T No 138

Name:	(*Macon*)
Manufacturer:	LBSCR, Brighton Works
Built:	1879
Running number:	138 (LBSCR), 2138 (SR), 32138 (BR)
At the docks:	1951

No 138 was dispatched from Brighton Works bearing the name *Macon* in January 1879, and was sent to work in New Cross where it seems to have led a fairly humdrum existence. By March 1929, it was stationed at Brighton, staying there for several years, but wartime service saw it transferred to Tonbridge by December 1943. It remained there until April 1949, after which it was at Nine Elms in April 1950. By March the following year, it had found its way to the docks as one of the customary E1 contingent before its days were numbered in October 1956.

LBSCR Class E1 0-6-0T No 151

Name:	(*Helvetia*)
Manufacturer:	LBSCR, Brighton Works
Built:	1880
Running number:	151 (LBSCR), 2151 (SR), 32151 (BR)
At the docks:	1959-1960

Built December 1880, and named *Helvetia*, this locomotive began its working life at New Cross, and spent most of its early career in that area. By March 1929, it was still assigned to New Cross, but by April 1932, it had made its way to Fratton as No 2151. On Nationalisation it became No 32151, and in November 1959, it was a regular at Southampton docks, just as several others of its class had been during the 1950s. It was there that it was condemned with fractured cylinders in January 1960.

Class E1 No 32113 passes Geddes Warehouse at the Town Quay en route to the Eastern Docks. (R.K. Blencowe Collection)

LBSCR No 138 still carries its name in pre-1905 livery. (D. Searle Collection)

Class E1 No 32151 finds time for a brief smoke alongside the Western Docks carriage shed on 30th July 1959. (R.K. Blencowe Collection)

LBSCR Class E1 0-6-0T No 606

Name:	(*Guernsey*)
Manufacturer:	LBSCR, Brighton Works
Built:	1876
Running number:	106 & 606 (LBSCR), 2606 (SR), 32606 (BR)
At the docks:	1950-1956

Built in October 1876, and carrying the name *Guernsey*, No 106 was initially based at Battersea. In April 1915, it had been renumbered to 606, its original number being allocated to an E2 class loco. By March 1929, it had been transferred to Brighton and was then at Fratton as Southern Railway No 2606 by April 1932. After Nationalisation it became 32606, and by April 1950, it had become allocated to Southampton Docks while based at Eastleigh, where it remained until taken out of service and scrapped in July 1956.

LBSCR Class E1 0-6-0T No 694

Name:	(*Cherbourg*)
Manufacturer:	LBSCR, Brighton Works
Built:	1875
Running number:	102, 694 (both LBSCR), 2694 (SR), 32694 (BR)
At the docks:	1953-1961

Built in March 1875, this loco left Brighton works as No 102 named *Cherbourg*, and was initially allocated duties the local area. It was then renumbered to 694 in October 1913, and by March 1929, it had been transferred to Fratton; a spell along the coast at Littlehampton followed in 1932. After World War II, No 694 was back at Fratton, and from August 1953, regular visits were made to Southampton Docks for turns of duty there until the end of the decade. Its final days were spent divided between Southampton, Eastleigh, Winchester and Portsmouth Dockyard as the last working example of its class before withdrawal came in July 1961. It was finally being broken up at Eastleigh in August that year.

LBSCR Class E2 0-6-0T No 100

Manufacturer:	LBSCR, at Brighton Works
Built:	1913
Running number:	100 (LBSCR), 2100 (SR), 32100 (BR)
At the docks:	1959 and 1961

Built in June 1913, No 100 was dispatched to Eastbourne, where it spent many years working goods trains and shunting the local sidings. It was then employed on motor trains running between London Bridge, Forest Hill and Crystal Palace, and at the formation of the Southern Railway (as No 2100), it was once again allocated to Eastbourne and thereafter to New Cross and Battersea. From 1936, it was employed shunting at Herne Hill and the Victoria area.

At Nationalisation, its number changed to 32100, and as electrification took place, many of the class were moved on in the latter 1950s, this loco being based at Eastleigh from where it found its way to the docks in December 1959. There it rotated duties with the other class members until being withdrawn from service in November 1961.

E1 class No 32606 seen at work in the Western Docks on 27th May 1956. (Tony Molyneaux / Kevin Robertson Collection)

E1 No 32694 at Southampton Docks in October 1960. (R.K. Blencowe Collection)

E2 Class B100 in early Southern days pictured at New Cross Gate. (R.K. Blencowe Collection)

LBSCR Class E2 0-6-0T No 101

Manufacturer:	LBSCR, at Brighton Works
Built:	1913
Running number:	101 (LBSCR), 2101 (SR), 32101 (BR)
At the docks:	1956 and 1961-1962

Built in June 1913, No 101 was sent to work at Battersea where it spent most of its active life. Having survived World War II and the Nationalisation of the railways, it was eventually transferred to Southampton docks via Eastleigh in December 1956, where it joined other class members 32108 and 32109 who had arrived there in the previous month. In latter years, all the E2s were based at Eastleigh and rotated for dock duty until, following the introduction of diesels, No 32101 was scrapped in September 1962.

LBSCR Class E2 0-6-0T No 102

Manufacturer:	LBSCR, at Brighton Works
Built:	1913
Running number:	102 (LBSCR), 2102 (SR), S2102 & 32102 (BR)
At the docks:	1959-1961

No 102 left Brighton works in August 1913, and began life in the local area until being transferred to Battersea in February 1919. There, it was employed with others of the class in running motor trains between London Bridge, Forest Hill and Crystal Palace. Southern Railway days found it still based at Battersea and engaged around Victoria for marshalling duties.

Under Nationalisation, it carried the number S2102 for a time, until receiving its full BR number. By December 1959, most of the class had been transferred to Eastleigh, from where they rotated duties at the docks, No 32102 taking its share until scrapped in October 1961.

LBSCR Class E2 0-6-0T No 103

Manufacturer:	LBSCR, at Brighton Works
Built:	1913
Running number:	103 (LBSCR), 2103 (SR), 32103 (BR)
At the docks:	1959-1962

December 1913 saw this locomotive leave the works for duties at New Cross, where it remained until Southern Railway days, but a coal strike in 1926 saw it pressed into service on passenger trains out of London Bridge. However, it was soon back to mundane shunting work at New Cross, and by 1936 it had moved to Battersea. It was transferred to Eastleigh in the late 1950s, and by December 1959, it was sharing docks duties with others of the class, until displaced by diesels and withdrawn from service in October 1962.

LBSCR Class E2 0-6-0T No 104

Manufacturer:	LBSCR, at Brighton Works
Built:	1914
Running number:	104 (LBSCR), 2104 (SR), 32104 (BR)
At the docks:	1959-1963

No 104 was the last of the original batch of E2s to leave Brighton works in January 1914, after which the remaining members of the class were built with modifications to the original design. It began its working life at New Cross, but after an unsuccessful period of operating motor trains out of London Bridge, it was transferred to Tunbridge Wells for similar duties, but with no greater fortune. It then returned to normal working at New Cross, where it remained until the Southern Railway grouping, when it was used briefly on passenger trains back at London Bridge during the 1926 coal strike; by 1936 it had been reallocated to Battersea.

As with all members of the class it survived into British Railways ownership, and by the late 1950s, had been transferred to Eastleigh, from where in December of that year it was sent to work in the docks with the other E2s. Dieselisation saw their demise, and along with No 32109, it was scrapped in April 1963, the pair being the final examples of their class.

E2 class No 32101 at Eastleigh shed on 3rd May 1958. (E.W. Fry / R.K. Blencowe Collection)

E2 No 32102 strikes an identical pose with 32101 (see above) at Eastleigh a decade earlier on 5th September 1948. (W. Gilburt / R.K. Blencowe Collection)

E2 No 32104 passes the Western Docks Engineer's Yard in March 1962. (L.F. Folkard)

LBSCR Class E2 0-6-0T No 105

Manufacturer:	LBSCR, at Brighton Works
Built:	1915
Running number:	105 (LBSCR), 2105 (SR), 32105 (BR)
At the docks:	1959 and 1961-1962

This locomotive was the first of the modified version of the class, and it left the works for Battersea in June 1915 where it handled local goods to Norwood Junction. By the middle of 1916, it had been transferred to Three Bridges, but it proved unpopular with the local crews and was soon sent back to its original haunts, where it remained into Southern Railway days. By early 1937, it had been sent to Dover where its dock duties included shunting sleeping cars for the train ferry. This engagement continued into the war years until France became occupied and cross channel services ceased. 2105 then returned to Battersea via a spell of shunting at Tonbridge.

As with others of this class, it was allocated to Eastleigh during the late 1950s, and from there it was regularly dispatched to work in the docks until withdrawn from service in September 1962.

LBSCR Class E2 0-6-0T No 106

Manufacturer:	LBSCR, at Brighton Works
Built:	1915
Running number:	106 (LBSCR), 2106 (SR), 32106 (BR)
At the docks:	1959 and 1961-1962

No 106 left the works having been completed in September 1915 after a delay due to the onset of World War I, and it was immediately sent for duty at New Cross where its principle task was piloting at London Bridge. Its schedule remained unaltered into Southern Railway days when New Cross was still its home base. The 1926 coal strike brought about a brief spell of passenger working, but otherwise, there was little change until most of the class were sent to Battersea, with the exception of Nos 2106 and 2107. These were both dispatched to Dover, where in 1936, they were occupied in shunting traffic for the train ferries until cross channel services were suspended. After a brief period of inactivity, the pair were sent to join the others at Battersea, via a short spell of shunting at Tonbridge.

After Nationalisation, the locomotive transferred to Eastleigh, eventually to work in Southampton docks, rotating duties from 1959 until the end of steam there in 1962, when 32106 lasted only until that October before being taken out of service and scrapped.

LBSCR Class E2 0-6-0T No 107

Manufacturer:	LBSCR, at Brighton Works
Built:	1916
Running number:	107 (LBSCR), 2107 (SR), 32107 (BR)
At the docks:	1956-1961

When built in March 1916, No 107 began work at New Cross where it spent most of its time piloting at London Bridge. Nothing much had changed by the 1923 grouping, but like Nos 103, 104 and 106, it was called upon to work passenger trains during the 1926 coal strike. It remained at New Cross until it was sent to work the train ferry stock at Dover in 1936 along with No 106, but after the cross channel service was withdrawn, their presence was no longer required.

When taken into British Railways it was transferred to Eastleigh, and by 1956, 32107 rotated shed duties with spells at Southampton Docks. This locomotive became the first of its class to be scrapped when it was withdrawn from service in February 1961.

E2 Class No 2106 in Southern days, at Stewarts Lane. (R.K. Blencowe Collection)

E2 No 32107 alongside the Western Docks carriage shed, in June 1960. (R.K. Blencowe Collection)

E2 No 32108 alongside the Western Docks carriage shed, in June 1960. (G. Stacey)

LBSCR Class E2 0-6-0T No 108

Manufacturer:	LBSCR, at Brighton Works
Built:	1916
Running number:	108 (LBSCR), 2108 (SR), 32108 (BR)
At the docks:	1956-1961

No 108 was the penultimate member of the class when it rolled out of the works in July 1916, and began work at Battersea, where it shared duties with No 105 on local goods trains to Norwood Junction. In Southern Railway days, as 2108, it continued at Battersea, from where in 1936 it was performing marshalling duties at Herne Hill and in the Victoria area. It accompanied 2109 to Hither Green in September 1942, remaining there until the pair was transferred to Ashford in January 1944. Little work was found for them and they were both sent off to Dover in the same year.

As BR No 32108 it was working freight between Eastbourne and Hastings during January 1953, and in November 1956, it accompanied 32109 to Eastleigh and thence to Southampton Docks in rotating duties. This was the final deployment of 32108 before withdrawal in June 1961, and being sent to the scrapheap.

LBSCR Class E2 0-6-0T No 109

Manufacturer:	LBSCR, at Brighton Works
Built:	1916
Running number:	109 (LBSCR), 2109 (SR), 32109 (BR)
At the docks:	1956-1962

E2 No 109 was the tenth and final member of the class to be built, and left Brighton works in October 1916. It immediately took up duties in its home town, where it remained until Southern Railway days, becoming No 2109. By 1926 it was on loan to Tunbridge Wells West, where it was employed on local passenger trains and goods services to Three Bridges. The mid 1930s saw it stationed at New Cross and then Battersea for shunting in the Victoria area. Together with No 2108, it was sent to Hither Green in December 1942 but their stay was short lived, and by January 1944 they had moved, first to Ashford, and then on to Dover by June of that same year.

This locomotive became British Railways No 32109 but, being no longer required at Dover, it was accompanied by 32108 to Eastleigh in November 1956. The two were sent to work in Southampton docks until steam working ended there, and its final days were spent at Eastleigh before withdrawal, as the last of the class, came in April 1963.

E2 No 32109 alongside the Western Docks carriage shed, in June 1960. (G. Stacey)

CHAPTER 5

Docks Engineer's Department 1928-1977

In addition to the locomotives engaged in full time dock duties, the Docks Engineer's Department retained engines for its own use. Such locos were never part of the general docks fleet, and were housed in the engineer's yard, primarily for general maintenance work. In the Eastern Docks, a yard was created just inside the main gate, on the east side of what is now Central Road, and the various buildings and workshops were contained within a small triangle of track that was often used to turn main line engines instead of sending them off to the Terminus turntable.

During the construction of the New (Western) Docks, a rather strange vehicle appeared on the scene. Officially classified as an F9 class 4-2-4T, it was an inspection saloon built in 1899 for the use of the LSWR Chief Mechanical Engineer, Dugald Drummond, and enabled him to tour various locations around the company network. After his death in 1912, it had been stored at Eastleigh, but from March 1932 it was recommissioned and sent to the docks to take parties of VIPs around the various works. On odd occasions, a trailing coach was added when visitor numbers demanded. This lasted until the docks extension was opened and *The Bug* (as was its uncomplimentary nickname) was sent back to Eastleigh, where it was eventually dismantled in 1940.

Once the New Docks were completed in 1935 a new, more spacious yard was laid out to the west of the carriage warming shed. The shed became the base for the four docks locos on duty at that end of the port but, in engineering matters, a separate locomotive was usually maintained in the yard and stored in the open, as there was no dedicated building to house it.

The first engine to fulfil this role was *The Master General*, an 0-4-0ST built in 1910 by Andrew Barclay, which arrived from the Mersey Docks and Harbour Board in April 1928 during the docks construction works.

McAlpine locomotive No 57, a Hudswell Clarke 0-6-0ST built in 1924, was employed on the widening of the Union Castle quaysides at berths 34, 35 and 36 in the Eastern Docks from May until October of 1939 (see Chapter 6). During this period it was loaned to the Engineer's Department during the month of June, presumably because *The Master General* was indisposed. (Confusingly, this loco exchanged numbers with McAlpine No 45 in 1933.)

The Master General continued in service at the yard until 1946, when it was replaced by a diesel loco (DS400) from the Royal Ordinance Factory in Aycliffe, County Durham. From then it was stored at Eastleigh until broken up in January 1949.

A small 2ft gauge diesel loco had been obtained from McAlpine in 1933 and converted to standard gauge. This outlived DS400, and remained in the yard until disposed of in 1977. It was the last of the dedicated docks engineering locos, and from that time, any departmental materials were moved by the shed allocated engines.

Looking across the Eastern Docks Engineer's Yard towards Central Road in July 1975. (Author)

LSWR F9 Class Inspection Saloon 4-2-4T No 733 *The Bug*

Manufacturer:	LSWR, Nine Elms Works
Built:	1899
Running numbers:	733 (LSWR) 58S (SR)
Cylinders:	11½in x 18in
Driving wheels:	5ft 7in
Working pressure:	175psi
Weight:	37 ton 8cwt (including saloon)
At the docks:	1932-1935

This vehicle was built in 1899 for the personal use of Chief Mechanical Engineer Dugald Drummond. In this grand little vehicle (unflatteringly called *The Bug* by employees) he also undertook tours of inspection around various works. After his death in 1912, the engine was placed in store at Nine Elms, but was transferred to Departmental Stock in December 1913 for the purpose of ferrying officials and VIPs around engineering projects.

By October 1916, it was back in storage, this time at Eastleigh, and it remained so until March 1932, when it was dispatched to Southampton Docks to take parties of dignitaries around the construction of the Western Docks. After the works were completed in 1935, it returned to storage at Eastleigh Works until August 1940 when it was dismantled. However, the saloon part survived as an Inspectors' hut at the Carriage Works until it was acquired by the Hampshire Narrow Gauge Railway Society in 1976 for use as a souvenir shop at its premises at Durley.

It was subsequently removed for preservation by the Drummond Society in January 1997 and is now being restored at the Swanage Railway.

F9 Class No 733 "The Bug" near the Royal Pier in 1932. The general debris will soon become Mayflower Park. (Associated British Ports)

McAlpine Contract Loco 0-6-0ST Hudswell Clarke No 1538

Name:	*Sir Robert McAlpine & Sons No 45*
Manufacturer:	Hudswell Clarke & Co Ltd, Leeds
Works number:	1538
Built:	1924
Running numbers:	57 (No 45 until 1933)
Cylinders:	13in x 20in
Driving wheels:	3ft 3½in
Wheelbase:	11ft 6in
Weight:	24ton 15cwt
At the docks:	1939

Upon arrival at Southampton in May 1939, No 57 became one of two locomotives employed by the contractors, McAlpine, during the widening of the Union Castle Line quayside in the Eastern Docks at berths 34, 35 and 36. This engine remained until October that year, but for a period during June it was loaned to the Docks Engineer's Department. Its time at there was followed by a return to McAlpine's Hayes depot, from where it was sold to John Mowlem & Co.

For more history of this engine, see "Union Castle Quays – McAlpine 1939" in Chapter 6.

Note: McAlpine locos No 45 and 57 swapped numbers in 1933, and although both locos worked at Southampton, they were there at different times and on different contracts.

Southern Railway Docks Engineer's Department 0-4-0ST Andrew Barclay No 1188

Name:	*The Master General*
Manufacturer:	Andrew Barclay & Sons, Kilmarnock
Works number:	1188
Built:	1911
Cylinders:	14in x 22in
Driving wheels:	3ft 5in
Wheelbase:	5ft 6in
Working pressure:	160psi
At the docks:	1928-1946

This loco was originally ordered by Vickers, Sons & Maxim Ltd of Barrow-in-Furness, and was to carry the name *Achilles*, but Vickers changed their requirements, and No 1188 was instead delivered new to the Royal Arsenal at Woolwich in February 1911. The loco began life there under a new name *The Master General* after the Master General of Ordnance. Later it worked at the Stanley Bros Brick and Tile Co Ltd at Stockingford, until it was purchased in the early 1920s by dealer Frank Edmunds, who carried out a major rebuild before selling it to the Mersey Docks & Harbour Board in January 1923.

At Liverpool it became MD&HB No 37, and among other duties, worked on the construction of the Gladstone Dock. When that project ended, it was sold to the Southern Railway for use in the Engineer's Department at Southampton Docks, arriving there in April 1928 for use in the New (later Western) Docks. There, it was stabled in the Engineer's Yard, working maintenance trains and hauling ballast around the new extension works.

By 1946, it had been replaced by a diesel loco and it was eventually transferred to Eastleigh, where it laid idle until scrapped in January 1949.

"The Master General", minus its name and work plates, pictured at Eastleigh during its final days in 1947. (Lens of Sutton)

CHAPTER 6

Docks Contractors 1886-1939

In the days before giant earth-movers and huge lorries, any significant amounts of soil and building equipment were moved around by rail. Much of the digging was done by steam shovel and, in the early days, a fair proportion by hand, with the extracted material being carried way in wagons hauled by a small army of railway engines.

If the life of an industrial tank engine can be described as "unglamorous", that of a contractor's locomotive must be the ultimate in drudgery. While many early photographs show immaculate engines and proud crews, the truth is that many were poorly maintained, having been purchased for a specific undertaking, ready to be written off the end of the scheme. Long hours of unrelenting duty would see many worked to a standstill before being patched up and moved to another contract, or simply thrown on the scrap heap. On other occasions, these proud little workhorses were exchanged or passed around between construction companies like worthless chattel, or sold off to new owners at base value to end their days rusting away on some long forsaken siding.

Because of the very nature of their gypsy-like existence, the lives of contractors' locomotives were often like shifting sands – you never knew where they might appear next. Written records from the past often contradict, and while new evidence is constantly being uncovered, some details are at times a little "sketchy" when it comes to plotting their histories. With this in mind I have attempted to compile the previous existences and the subsequent fortunes of all of those that served their time at Southampton Docks, and I trust the reader will forgive any omissions.

Since the establishment of Southampton Docks in 1842, many huge engineering works were involved in its various major expansions. Each of these took several years to complete, and during those periods of construction, large numbers of locomotives were stationed in the docks for the length of the contract. Although they were never permanently allocated to the docks, in most instances they gave years of commendable service there before, in many cases, fading into obscurity.

Contract **Page**

Construction of the King George V Graving Dock was well advanced when this photograph featuring two of Mowlem's locomotives was taken. The locomotive at the bottom right is either Andrew Barclay "Shirley" or "Witham". (Associated British Ports)

Empress Dock – S. Pearson & Son, 1886-1890

The Southampton Dock Company carried out the early extensions to the Itchen Quays in the 1870s with its own locos, but the first major expansion, the building of the Empress Dock, was given to contactors S. Pearson & Son, who spent four years on the project from 1886 to 1890. During this period, Pearsons employed at least four locos named *Solent*, *Gipsy*, *Harold* and *Southampton*.

The newly completed dock covered 18½ acres, with over 3,500 feet of quays, and was opened by Queen Victoria on 26th July 1890. At that time, it was the only dock in Britain where vessels of the deepest draught could enter at any state of the tide.

Celebrations at the opening of the Empress Dock. (Southampton City Archive)

Pearson Contract Loco 0-4-0ST Hunslet No 387

Name:	*Gipsy*
Manufacturer:	Hunslet Engine Co Ltd, Hunslet, Leeds
Works number:	387
Built:	1886
Cylinders:	9in x 14in
Driving wheels:	2ft 8½in
Wheelbase:	4ft 6in
Weight:	12ton 0cwt
At the docks:	1886-1890

Gipsy arrived new from the makers in 1886, and began work for Pearsons at Southampton's Empress Dock. After completion of the works, it was transferred to the Blackwall Tunnel contract at Rotherhithe, London, where it worked from 1890-7.

Little further is known, except that in later years it was sold to the Tilbury Contracting & Dredging Co, where it was employed at the East Tilbury rubbish tip until scrapped in 1953.

Pearson Contract Loco 0-6-0ST Hunslet No 400

Name:	*Harold*
Manufacturer:	Hunslet Engine Co Ltd, Hunslet, Leeds
Works number:	400
Built:	1886
Cylinders:	11in x 15in
Driving wheels:	2ft 6in
Wheelbase:	9ft 6in
Weight:	15ton 10cwt
At the docks:	1886-1890

Harold arrived new from the makers to work on the construction of the Empress Dock in July 1886. After completion, it was transferred to Chesterfield, where it was employed on the Chesterfield to Warsop line in Derbyshire/Nottinghamshire, before moving on to another railway project for the Langwith to Beighton line in the same area between 1892 and 1897.

Then came employment on the Wootton Bassett to Patchway line for the GWR from 1897 to 1902, with a move to the Queens Dock branch at Liverpool in 1902-3, before finding its way to the King George V Dock at Hull between 1906 and 1914.

Wartime service saw a transfer to the Ministry of Munitions Filling Factory at Crossgates, Leeds, where it lost its name, before arriving at its final location at the Stourton Quarries of the Leeds Sand & Gravel Co, where it ended its days. Nothing more is recorded about *Harold* but the site was closed about 1930.

Pearson Contract Loco 0-4-0ST Manning Wardle No 882

Name:	*Solent*
Manufacturer:	Manning Wardle & Co Ltd, Hunslet, Leeds
Works number:	882
Built:	1883
Cylinders:	10in x 16in
Driving wheels:	2ft 9in
Wheelbase:	4ft 9in
Weight:	15ton 0cwt
At the docks:	1886-1890

This locomotive was delivered new in April 1883 to Kirk & Randall's contract at Tilbury Dock, Essex, where it carried the number 23. It was afterwards sold to S. Pearson & Son who named it *Solent* and employed it on the construction of the Empress Dock.

After completion of the work there, it was sold to Baldry & Yerburgh in 1892 and used on their Kirkby in Ashfield to Langwith contract in 1894, carrying the name *Morecambe* until sold once more to Godfrey & Liddlow.

It was subsequently recorded as working for D. Shanks on the Otterington widening contract, in Yorkshire, and was later offered for sale in March 1899. From then, it was employed by J. Phillips & Co during construction of the Gifford & Garvald Light Railway from 1899 until 1901 as their loco No 2. In October 1901, the loco was advertised for sale, when it appears to have been taken by dealers J.H. Riddle, who themselves advertised it a month later. Nothing further is known.

Pearson Contract Loco 0-6-0ST Hunslet No 407

Name:	*Southampton*
Manufacturer:	Hunslet Engine Co Ltd, Hunslet, Leeds
Works number:	407
Built:	1886
Cylinders:	15in x 20in
Driving wheels:	3ft 4in
Wheelbase:	12ft 0in
Weight:	29ton 0cwt
At the docks:	1886-1890

Arriving new from the makers in October 1886, S*outhampton* began its working life at the Empress Dock construction works. After completion of the dock, it was sold in 1897, via the firm of R.H. Robinson of Derby, to A.M. Mundy at Shipley Colliery, Derbyshire, ending its days there when scrapped in September 1925.

White Star Dock – Topham, Jones & Railton, 1908-1911

The next vast development came in the LSWR years when Messrs Topham, Jones and Railton were engaged to build the White Star Dock (now the Ocean Dock). Following exploratory excavations by the dock authority, the company was awarded the contract in October 1907, and the project employed no less than twelve locomotives between 1908 and 1911, the majority of these having been built by Manning Wardle, whose engines were stalwarts of the industrial railway world.

This dock, covering some 15½ acres, was not the largest of the four basins, but was certainly the deepest, with a clearance of 40ft at low water. Initially built to accommodate the vessels of the White Star Line, which transferred its operations from Liverpool in 1907, it was first used in June 1911 and eventually became home to the world's greatest liners.

Constructing the White Star Dock in 1908. (Southampton City Archive)

Trafalgar Drydock – Topham, Jones & Railton, 1911-1913

Construction of the Trafalgar Graving Dock (later No 6 Drydock) commenced in August 1901, and was carried out by contractors John Aird & Co, who had been associated with various works in Southampton Docks for at least a decade beforehand, although there is no record of their locomotives being used in these projects. The dock was opened in October 1905, but due to the tremendous growth in the size of ships it was soon outdated, and the need for larger accommodation became a pressing issue. As a new drydock would have taken about five years to construct, it was decided to enlarge this most recent structure. The firm of Topham James & Railton was already engaged in building the White Star Dock, and they were given the immediate task of carrying out widening works to the Trafalgar Graving Dock which lasted until its reopening in April 1913.

TJR locos *Chagford*, *Pereyra*, *Test*, *Worsley* and *Wymondley* were engaged in these works.

Topham Contract Locomotive 0-4-0ST Manning Wardle No 1087

Name:	*Chagford*
Manufacturer:	Manning Wardle & Co Ltd, Hunslet, Leeds
Works number:	1087
Built:	1889
Running number:	35
Cylinders:	9in x 14in
Driving wheels:	2ft 9in
Wheelbase:	4ft 9in
Weight:	11ton 0cwt
At the docks:	1908-1913

This locomotive was supplied new to J.E. Billup of Newbury in July 1889 to work on the Lambourne Valley Railway, from which it took its original name of *Lambourne*. When the contractor went broke in June 1890, ownership was transferred to the railway company until given over to another contractor S. Pearson & Son who saw completion of the line.

The loco then passed to the firm of James & John Dickson, where it was renamed *Chagford* during the construction of the GWR Exeter to Christow line between 1894 and 1903. Ownership then passed to Topham, Jones & Railton Ltd, who were working on the Kings Dock contract at Swansea, before its arrival at Southampton Docks in 1908, where it was one of many locomotives employed by Topham during the construction of the White Star Dock and widening of the Trafalgar Graving Dock.

After leaving Southampton around 1913, it was later employed by Topham at the Admiralty Harbour works in Invergordon, which lasted from 1913 to 1919, and by 1923-1924 was engaged at the Surrey Commercial Docks extension for the Port of London Authority.

By February 1930, *Chagford* had arrived at the Blaenclydach Colliery in South Wales, possibly via Topham's nearby Swansea Depot, and there it remained in service until scrapped in April 1935.

Topham Contract Locomotive 0-6-0ST Manning Wardle No 1033

Name:	*Ditton*
Manufacturer:	Manning Wardle & Co Ltd, Hunslet, Leeds
Works number:	1033
Built:	1888
Running number:	10
Cylinders:	12in x 17in
Driving wheels:	3ft 1½in
Wheelbase:	10ft 9in
Weight:	18ton 10cwt
At the docks:	1908-1911

After being supplied new to T.A. Walker at Runcorn in January 1888 for works on the Manchester Ship Canal, this locomotive became one of several purchased from that location in 1894 by contractors Topham, Jones, and Railton Ltd, and used during the construction of the Aylestone to Rugby line contract in Leicestershire until 1898.

Taking the name *Ditton*, it was subsequently employed by Topham on the construction of the White Star Dock. After work at the dock was completed, it was stationed at the company's Crymlyn Burrows depot, Swansea until March 1918, when it transferred to another Topham contract for the construction of the Oxfordshire Ironstone Co Mineral Railway at Wroxton, remaining there until returning to Swansea in March 1919.

Subsequent labours saw employment on the Port of London Authority extension to the Surrey Commercial Docks between 1923 and 1924, and afterwards, *Ditton* was sold to the Royal Ordnance Factory at Rotherwas, Herefordshire, finally going to E.O. Edwards at Chesterfield for scrap in 1946.

Topham Contract Locomotive 0-4-0ST Manning Wardle No 716

Name:	*Guston*
Manufacturer:	Manning Wardle & Co Ltd, Hunslet, Leeds
Works number:	716
Built:	1878
Running number:	11
Cylinders:	10in x 16in
Driving wheels:	2ft 9in
Wheelbase:	4ft 9in
Weight:	15ton 0cwt
At the docks:	1908-1911

After being delivered new to T.A. Walker in December 1878 to work on the construction of the Manchester Ship Canal, this loco was one of a number purchased from there by Topham, Jones, and Railton Ltd in 1894, and was employed on the Aylestone to Rugby line contract in Leicestershire. *Guston* remained there until 1898, before becoming one of several locomotives used by Topham during the construction of the White Star Dock.

After the docks project was completed, *Guston* was subsequently employed from 1915 at the Kirton-in-Lindsey works of the Caustic Lime & Macadam Co Ltd in Lincolnshire, until it was scrapped there around 1925.

"Guston" and crew pose for the camera at Cosby in Leicestershire while working on the Aylestone to Rugby line in 1897. (S.W.A. Newton / Leicester Museum)

Topham Contract Locomotive 0-4-0ST Hudswell Clarke No 599

Name:	*Haddenham*
Manufacturer:	Manning Wardle & Co Ltd, Hunslet, Leeds
Works number:	599
Built:	1902
Running number:	32
Cylinders:	10in x 16in
Driving wheels:	2ft 9½in
Wheelbase:	5ft 6in
Weight:	15ton 15cwt
At the docks:	1908-1911

This locomotive was new to L.P. Nott in October 1902 and was employed on their Princes Risborough – Grendon Underwood contract in Buckinghamshire. It was then sold to Topham, Jones & Railton for their Kings Dock Contract at Swansea, before its arrival at Southampton for the construction of the White Star Dock from 1908. Little else is known about this loco after work was completed at Southampton, but it was later reported as working for Nott, Brodie & Co Ltd on the Avonmouth Portway contract at Bristol in 1921.

Topham Contract Locomotive 0-4-0ST Manning Wardle No 1042

Name:	*Pereyra*
Manufacturer:	Manning Wardle & Co Ltd, Hunslet, Leeds
Works number:	1042
Built:	1887
Running number:	37
Cylinders:	12in x 18in
Driving wheels:	3ft 0in
Wheelbase:	5ft 4in
Weight:	19ton 10cwt
At the docks:	1908 - 1913

Pereyra was delivered new to T.A. Walker in January 1888 and shipped for contract works in Buenos Aires before returning home to employment by C.H. Walker at Sudbrook Shipyard, Gwent. It was afterwards purchased by Topham, Jones & Railton in April 1908 for use during the construction of the White Star Dock, and afterwards, the widening of the Trafalgar Graving Dock.

It was rebuilt by Topham in 1914, and there is no further record of its activities until, by August 1928, it had been sold to the Tyne Improvement Commission at South Shields, where it saw service until being scrapped in June 1949.

"Pereyra" at the South Pier Works, South Shields, working for the Tyne Improvement Trust in July 1933. (L.G. Charlton Collection)

Topham Contract Locomotive 0-4-0ST Peckett No 439

Name:	*Phoenix*
Manufacturer:	Peckett & Sons, Bristol
Works number:	439
Built:	1885
Running number:	14
Cylinders:	10in x 14in
Driving wheels:	2ft 6in
Wheelbase:	5ft 0in
Working pressure:	125psi
At the docks:	1908-1911

The locomotive was originally supplied in January 1885 to Daniel Edwards & Co, but almost immediately it was returned to the builders before being resold to James Evans of Birmingham, who were engaged in the construction of the Parkgate Junction to West Kirby line until 1886. The loco had acquired the name *Bristol* by the time it was sold to contractors Meakin and Dean of Birkenhead, who worked on various sections of the Wirral Railway until 1895.

During this period, the loco appears to have been subcontracted to Thomas W. Davies in August 1893, after which disaster struck the following January when the boiler exploded, killing the driver and fireman. After repairs had been carried out, it was sold to Topham, Jones and Railton who gave it the running number 14 and the appropriate new name of *Phoenix* when engaged in the Kings Dock contract at Swansea. It arrived at Southampton in 1908, where it was employed on the construction of the White Star Dock.

After work was completed at Southampton, *Phoenix* was purchased by contractor H. Lovatt of Wolverhampton, before a spell of duties with her final owners at the Dulais Tinplate Factory, Pontardulais. The factory closed and was dismantled in March 1946. Presumably, *Phoenix* met the same fate.

There are several remarkable coincidences between Peckett 439 and her sister engine 438 in that both worked at tinplate factories in Pontardulais, both suffered boiler explosions, and both spent some time in Southampton, where 438 was occupied for several years on the Chapel Tramway (see Chapter 13).

See page 143 for an illustration of a typical Peckett M3 design.

Topham Contract Locomotive 0-4-0ST Manning Wardle No 1088

Name:	*Sankey*
Manufacturer:	Manning Wardle & Co Ltd, Hunslet, Leeds
Works number:	1088
Built:	1888
Running number:	12
Cylinders:	10in x 16in
Driving wheels:	2ft 9in
Wheelbase:	4ft 9in
Weight:	14ton 10cwt
At the docks:	1908-1911

Completed in December 1888, *Sankey* was purchased for work on the Manchester Ship Canal by contractor T.A. Walker who employed over a hundred locomotives in the project. This locomotive subsequently worked on the Aylestone to Rugby line contract in Leicestershire between 1894 and 1898. It then went on hire to S. Pearson & Sons, who were engaged in the construction of Seaham South Dock between 1899 and 1907. A spell at their Dover Harbour Breakwater contract followed, prior to *Sankey* becoming one of several locomotives employed by Topham, Jones, and Railton Ltd during the construction of the White Star Dock.

After work at Southampton was completed it spent time at the Crymlyn Burrows depot, Swansea, and in October 1917, was transferred to another Topham contract for the construction of the Oxfordshire Ironstone Co Ltd Mineral Railway at Wroxton, until returning to Swansea in April 1918. It is then thought to have been purchased by the Edge Hill Light Railway in Warwickshire in June 1922. That railway closed in 1925, after which *Sankey* remained out of use until finally broken up in 1946.

"St Andrews" pictured in 1897 at Lutterworth, Leicestershire. (S.W.A. Newton / Leicester Museum)

Topham Contract Locomotive 0-6-0ST Manning Wardle No 1012

Name:	*St Andrews*
Manufacturer:	Manning Wardle & Co Ltd, Hunslet, Leeds
Works number:	1012
Built:	1887
Running number:	5
Cylinders:	12in x 17in
Driving wheels:	3ft 1½in
Wheelbase:	10ft 9in
Weight:	18ton 10cwt
At the docks:	1908-1911

This locomotive was supplied new to T.A. Walker in June 1887 for their Manchester Ship Canal contract. After being purchased by Topham, Jones, and Railton in 1894, it was one of several locomotives employed by them on the Aylestone to Rugby line contract in Leicestershire that ended in 1898.

By 1908, it was employed on the construction of the White Star Dock, and after work there was completed, further service was given on the Logan & Hemmingway contract for the Sandy Lodge to Watford Metropolitan Line in 1923, but no later details are recorded for this loco.

See page 61 for an illustration of this locomotive.

Topham Contract Locomotive 0-4-0ST Avonside No 1509

Name:	*Test*
Manufacturer:	Avonside Engine Co Ltd, Bristol
Works number:	1509
Built:	1907
Running number:	28
Cylinders:	12in x 18in
Driving wheels:	2ft 10¾in
Wheelbase:	5ft 0in
At the docks:	1909-1913

Supplied new to Topham, Jones & Railton in September 1907, this locomotive worked on the King's Dock project at Swansea, and as *Test*, was one of a number of locos employed during the construction of the White Star Dock and the widening of the Trafalgar Dry Dock. Further employment took this loco back to Swansea in July 1913 for sea wall repairs at the Kings Dock, and then to the Fishguard Harbour breakwater by June 1914.

Test made an appearance at the Royal Dockyard, Pembroke in February 1920, and was rebuilt by Topham during that year at their Crymlyn Burrows plant depot at Swansea before being sold to Straker & Love's Brancepeth Colliery, County Durham in December 1920. There it took the name *Willington* after its new location, and then it moved to Brandon Colliery in October of the following year. A final transfer to the NCB No 5 area in mid-west Durham came in January 1947, this being its ultimate location until being scrapped in November 1953.

Topham Contract Locomotive 0-6-0ST Hudswell Clarke No 325

Name:	*Worsley*
Manufacturer:	Hudswell Clarke & Co Ltd, Leeds
Works number:	325
Built:	1889
Running number:	4
Cylinders:	13in x 20in
Driving wheels:	3ft 3in
Weight:	18ton 0cwt
At the docks:	1908-1913

This loco originally worked for T.A. Walker, having been supplied new for the construction of the Manchester Ship Canal. It was sold to Topham, Jones and Railton in 1894, and worked on the Aylestone to Rugby railway, which was completed in 1899. It was next employed at the Queen Alexandra Dock, Cardiff and then at the Kings Dock at Swansea from 1904, until arriving at Southampton in 1908 for the construction of the White Star Dock. There it also saw use in the widening of the Trafalgar Graving Dock. Its next assignment was to the Admiralty Harbour works at Invergordon, which ran from 1913 to 1919, and by 1923, it was found working on the Port of London Authority's extension to Surrey Commercial Docks until 1924, when it was offered for sale in April of that year. It is believed to have been purchased by C.J. Wills & Sons Ltd, but this has yet to be established and no further record exists.

CONTRACTORS – WHITE STAR DOCK AND TRAFALGAR DRY DOCK

"Test" at Straker & Love's Brandon Colliery in August 1952. (L.G. Charlton)

"Worsley" takes a break at Shawell, Leicestershire in March 1897. (S.W.A. Newton / Leicester Museum)

Topham Contract Locomotive 0-4-0ST Manning Wardle No 1343

Name:	(*Westminster*)
Manufacturer:	Manning Wardle & Co Ltd, Hunslet, Leeds
Works number:	1343
Built:	1897
Running number:	29
Cylinders:	10in x 16in
Driving wheels:	2ft 9in
Wheelbase:	4ft 9in
Weight:	16ton 0cwt
At the docks:	1910-1911

This loco was supplied new in June 1897 to Pauling & Co as their No 11 for work on the Stert Junction to Westbury line contract which ran until 1900. It was subsequently reported as working for Robert T. Relf & Son on the Fareham to Alton line contract, before employment by C.J. Wills & Sons on the Castle Cary to Langport works.

In 1908, it had been sold to Topham, Jones and Railton Ltd, who rebuilt the loco in 1910, and employed it on the building of the White Star Dock. This loco was their No 29 and was normally referred to by the name *Westminster*, although some sources say this word was only carried on the locomotive's tanks as part of the address of a previous owner. Nevertheless, it seems odd that this would be the only unnamed engine on the Southampton contract.

Westminster was next recorded working for C. & A. Walker at the Midland Ironworks at Donnington, Shropshire, having moved there from Topham in 1914. There it remained until it was sent to the Minworth Disposal Depot of H. Bridges in Warwickshire, where it was scrapped in 1952.

Topham Contract Locomotive 0-6-0ST Manning Wardle No 1331

Name:	*Wymondley*
Manufacturer:	Manning Wardle & Co Ltd, Hunslet, Leeds
Works number:	1331
Built:	1897
Running number:	30
Cylinders:	12in x 18in
Driving wheels:	3ft 0in
Wheelbase:	10ft 9in
Weight:	19ton 10cwt
At the docks:	1908-1913

Wymondley was delivered new from the makers to contractors C. Baker at Wymondley in April 1897. They immediately employed it on widening works between Stevenage and Hitchin during that year, before selling the loco on to Robert T. Relf for use on the Fareham to Alton line between 1898 and 1903. Another sale to C.J. Wills at Henley-in-Arden had taken place before *Wymondley* eventually found its way to Topham, Jones & Railton in 1906. It worked on the construction of the Kings Dock, Swansea before being engaged in the building of the White Star Dock from 1908 to 1911, and subsequently on the alterations to the Trafalgar Graving Dock from 1911 to 1913.

Between 1918 and 1920, Topham employed the loco on their Admiralty contract at Inverkeithing, but by June 1921, it had been shipped abroad for work on the Jahore Causeway in Malaya, before returning home for engagement on the Port of London Authority extension to the Surrey Commercial Docks in 1923-4. It then spent time at Topham's Swansea depot before being sold in 1927 to Perry & Co (Bow) Ltd, who used the loco on works for the Bromborough Docks in Cheshire. By July 1929, this much-travelled loco had reportedly found another new owner, this time being contractor John H. Wilson at Birkenhead, but that move is not confirmed and no further activities are known.

Western Docks – McAlpine 1927-1934

On assuming control of the docks in 1923 the Southern Railway embarked on the biggest project in the port's history, that of building the New (Western) Docks between 1927 and 1934. The main contractor for this immense task was Sir Robert McAlpine & Sons, who engaged no less than 19 locos on these works, mainly from Hudswell Clarke.

To facilitate movement of materials, the railway to the Town Quay was extended past the Royal Pier to a reclaimed area that was to become the bridgehead for the storage and distribution of supplies. This area was later to become the Mayflower Park.

The completed quay wall stretched over 7,500 feet in length and could simultaneously accommodate eight of the world's largest vessels, the depth of water being some 45 feet at low water. Along the frontage were some 41 cranes serving eight large transit sheds, each 150 feet wide. These were built in pairs with integral waiting halls and rail facilities for rapid passenger handling.

The New Docks construction heads across West Bay. Note the remains of the World War I Train Ferry jetty (see Chapter 9). (Associated British Ports)

Herbert Walker Avenue in the New Docks. One of McAlpine's locos is hauling a train of railway company wagons. (Associated British Ports)

Right: In conjunction with the docks construction scheme, a new viaduct was built over the Millbrook end of Southampton West Station to alleviate road traffic congestion on the original level crossing. The photograph shows a McAlpine locomotive with a rake of SR open wagons during the works on the 10th May 1934. (ILS Collection)

Left: Another McAlpine loco sits on the corner of the initial works site. (Author's Collection)

McAlpine Contract Locomotive 0-6-0ST Hudswell Clarke No 492

Name:	*Sir Robert McAlpine & Sons No 9*
Manufacturer:	Hudswell Clarke & Co Ltd, Leeds
Works number:	492
Built:	1898
Running number:	9
Cylinders:	12in x 18in
Driving wheels:	3ft 0in
Weight:	18ton 0cwt
At the docks:	1928-1934

No 9 was supplied new to Robert McAlpine & Sons at Glasgow for work on the Mallaig Railway from 1898 to 1900 (where it took the name *Mallaig*, carrying it until March 1917). From then there were spells at Provan Gasworks (1900-03) and the Culter Reservoir (1903-06). During World War I, the loco saw service at the Loch Doon School of Aerial Gunnery (1917-18) before moving to the National Spelter Works at Avonmouth after hostilities ceased. It was subsequently employed at various works at Slough (1919-20), Queenborough (1920-21) and Dartford (1922-23). This locomotive was rebuilt by Hudswell Clarke in 1923, before further employment on the St Lawrence to Ramsgate line (1925-26), and at Ellesmere Port on the Manchester Ship Canal (1926-7).

On arrival at Southampton Docks in 1928, it was used until completion of the contract and sent to the McAlpine depot at Hayes in March 1934, where it was stationed for a couple of years until moving on to the Hollowell Reservoir (1936-38) and Scunthorpe Steelworks (1938-40) before returning to Hayes, and being sold to John Mowlem & Co in January 1940.

Mowlem's used the loco during construction of the Swynnerton Royal Ordnance Factory in Staffordshire during World War II, where it took the name *Stafford*, after which it returned to the company's London Depot at Welham Green in 1942. No further use is recorded, and by September 1950, the loco had been partially dismantled, and had disappeared completely after August 1951.

See page 69 for an illustration of this locomotive.

McAlpine Contract Locomotive 0-6-0ST Hudswell Clarke No 888

Name:	*Sir Robert McAlpine & Sons No 26*
Manufacturer:	Hudswell Clarke & Co Ltd, Leeds
Works number:	888
Built:	1909
Running number:	26
Cylinders:	15in x 20in
Driving wheels:	3ft 7in
Wheelbase:	10ft 9in
Weight:	32ton 0cwt
At the docks:	1929-1934

No 26 was supplied new to Sir Robert McAlpine and Sons at Methil Docks in August 1909, and worked there until 1912 before moving to the Great Northern Railway site at Cuffley. It remained there until 1915, after which came a transfer to British Dyes, Huddersfield. After 6 years at the dye works, there followed visits to Dalmuir (1921), then to the St Lawrence to Ramsgate Railway (1926) before two years service on the Tilbury Docks contract.

During 1927 the locomotive was rebuilt by Hudswell Clarke, and after moving from Tilbury to Southampton in 1928 for work on the New Docks, it would appear the loco might have proved troublesome, as it was put up for sale in October 1929. Any problems must have been resolved, as No 26 continued working until the end of the Southampton contract, and then was engaged in further employment at the Guest Keen Baldwin Steelworks at their East Moors works in Cardiff from 1934 until April 1936, when it was eventually sold to them and became their No 14. By 1949, it had been transferred to the steel company's Dowlais works where it remained until scrapped in 1956.

McAlpine Contract Locomotive 0-6-0ST Hudswell Clarke No 1011

Name:	*Sir Robert McAlpine & Sons No 30*
Manufacturer:	Hudswell Clarke & Co Ltd, Leeds
Works number:	1011
Built:	1912
Running number:	30
Cylinders:	15in x 20in
Driving wheels:	3ft 7in
Wheelbase:	10ft 9in
Weight:	32ton 0cwt
At the docks:	1932-1934

Supplied new to Sir Robert McAlpine & Sons, this locomotive began work on the Cuffley to Hertford Railway in November 1912, where it remained until 1916. There followed a number of postings at Loch Doon School of Aerial Gunnery (1917-8), Turnberry Aerodrome (1918-9), Normanby (1921), Watling Street, Dartford (1922-4), St. Lawrence–Ramsgate Railway (1926) and Tilbury Docks from 1926 until 1929, before arrival at Southampton in April 1932.

After leaving the docks in October 1934 it was employed at the GKB steelworks at Cardiff until 1936, and then at Ebbw Vale (1936-8), before spending a couple of years at McAlpine's Hayes depot. In October 1940, it was sold to the Appleby-Frodingham Steel Co at their Cringle Ironstone Pits, where it ran as No 14. It then had spells at Colsterworth East Ironstone Mines in 1944, and in 1951-2, before eventually being scrapped in April 1958.

No 9 at McAlpine's Hayes Depot on 28th January 1939. (G. Alliez)

Former McAlpine No 26 in later life at the East Moors works of British (GKB) Iron & Steel Co on 19th June 1937. (B.D. Stoyel)

No 30 at work in the New (Western) Docks in the early 1930s. (G. Alliez)

McAlpine Contract Locomotive 0-6-0ST Hudswell Clarke No 1028

Name:	*Sir Robert McAlpine & Sons No 32*
Manufacturer:	Hudswell Clarke & Co Ltd, Leeds
Works number:	1028
Built:	1913
Running number:	32
Cylinders:	12in x 18in
Driving wheels:	3ft 1in
Wheelbase:	10ft 6in
Weight:	21ton 10cwt
At the docks:	1929–1931 and 1939

No 32 arrived new to Sir Robert McAlpine & Sons for work on the construction of the Cuffley-Hertford Railway in May 1913, where it saw three years service prior to a visit to the National Spelter Works at Avonmouth in 1918-19. Then followed two years at Dolgarog, Llyn Cowlyd, until moving to the Hayes Housing Project in 1921.

After a stopover at McAlpine's Great Stanney Depot, it was sent to Watling Street, Dartford in 1922 until September of the following year. 1925 saw further employment at Ellesmere Port on the Manchester Ship Canal, which lasted for two years until joining the contract at Tilbury Docks in 1927. Another two-year stint followed at the West India Dock, before its first arrival at Southampton in May 1929.

It left the docks in July 1931, and was laid up at the Great Stanney and Hayes depots, before resuming labours at the Cheddar Reservoir until November 1933, after which it worked at the Mogden Sewage Works until April 1935.

Following another stopover at Hayes depot from April 1935 until July 1936, it found its way back to Southampton in January 1939 as the first of two locomotives employed during the widening of the Union Castle Line Quays at berths 34, 35 and 36 in the Eastern Docks.

Its return to the Hayes depot in December 1939 lasted a month before transfer to Dalbeattie in January 1940, working there until February 1941, when it was idle for a year back at Hayes. It was then placed on hire to the GKB Steelworks at Cardiff from February to April 1942, after which it was hired out again, this time to the Gramophone Company at Hayes. That engagement lasted from June 1942 until January 1943, when it made its final return to McAlpine's depot at Hayes. It remained in storage there until sold to the Hards Motor Co for scrap in July 1956.

HC 1028 at McAlpine's Yard, Hayes on 29th October 1955. (J.P. Mullett)

McAlpine Contract Locomotive 0-6-0ST Hudswell Clarke No 1029

Name:	*Sir Robert McAlpine & Sons No 33*
Manufacturer:	Hudswell Clarke & Co Ltd, Leeds
Works number:	1029
Built:	1913
Running number:	33
Cylinders:	12in x 18in
Driving wheels:	3ft 1in
Wheelbase:	10ft 6in
Weight:	21ton 10cwt
At the docks:	1929–1933

No 33 arrived new from the makers (along with sister loco HC 1028) to work on the Cuffley-Hertford railway contract of Sir Robert McAlpine & Sons in May 1913. After three years there, it was transferred to British Dyes at Huddersfield for a year's labour in 1916-17. In 1918, it found itself at the British Cellulose factory, Spondon, Derby, until October of that year, after which it appeared at the Wilbraham Estate in Manchester in 1921. It was subsequently moved south and arrived at Tilbury Docks in November 1926, where it was engaged until April 1929 before being sent to join the ever growing McAlpine fleet during the construction of Southampton's New (Western) Docks.

There it stayed until 1933, and it was next employed at the GKB steelworks in Cardiff from June the following year. From there, it moved to the Southern Railway works on the Chessington Line in 1935. Leaving there in 1936, it had further calls at both the Cheddar and Hollowell Reservoirs during the same year, before enjoying a short rest at the Hayes depot in 1937. However, in December that year it was off again to the Appleby Frodingham Steel Co at Scunthorpe for two years before returning to Hayes once more.

There then followed a brief loan period to George Wimpey at Park Royal, before being sold to another branch of the McAlpine empire (Alfred) in June 1941. By January 1947, it had been sold again (via G. Cohen) to the National Coal Board, where it was based at Radstock for duties at the Norton Hill Somerset Collieries, until its final sale to the firm of C. Whitlock at Wapping Wharf, Bristol for scrap in February 1951.

McAlpine's No 33 with running mates at Southampton Docks on 25th September 1932. (H.F. Wheeller)

McAlpine Contract Locomotive 0-6-0ST Hudswell Clarke No 1526

Name:	*Sir Robert McAlpine & Sons No 41*
Manufacturer:	Hudswell Clarke & Co Ltd, Leeds
Works number:	1526
Built:	1924
Running number:	41
Cylinders:	12in x 18in
Driving wheels:	3ft 1in
Wheelbase:	10ft 6in
Weight:	21ton 10cwt
At the docks:	1929-1931

No 41 was delivered new to Sir Robert McAlpine & Son at Oldbury in April 1924, and was subsequently employed on the Birmingham to Wolverhampton Road works until 1926, when it was transferred to Tilbury Docks in October of that year. At the end of its stay there, in August 1928, it was sent to the Great Stanney Depot until called to Southampton in November 1929.

Employment at Southampton lasted until 1931, when another move saw its appearance at Stanlow Oil Dock on the Manchester Ship Canal, followed by work at Elderslie Dock from May 1932, until transfer to Wallsend Drydock in 1933. From there, in 1934, it spent two years at the Great Stanney Depot before moving to Ebbw Vale from 1936 to 1938. Spells of inactivity at both Great Stanney and Hayes followed before it was sold to Samuel Williams & Sons at Dagenham Dock in March 1940 (after overhaul at the engineering works of Abelson & Co) where it was gainfully employed until finally scrapped in 1957.

Former McAlpine No 41 pictured on 27th April 1957 as Samuel Williams No 10 at Dagenham Dock. (53A Models of Hull Collection)

McAlpine Contract Locomotive 0-6-0ST Hudswell Clarke No 1513

Name:	*Sir Robert McAlpine & Sons No 42*
Manufacturer:	Hudswell Clarke & Co Ltd, Leeds
Works number:	1513
Built:	1924
Running number:	42
Cylinders:	13in x 20in
Driving wheels:	3ft 3½in
Wheelbase:	11ft 6in
Weight:	24ton 15cwt
At the docks:	1929-1931

No 42 was delivered new in March 1924 to Sir Robert McAlpine & Sons at Garsadden (via the Singer Sewing Machine Company) for construction work on the Anniesland-Duntocher Road, after which it was employed on the Watford Bypass in the same year before transfer to the Birmingham to Wolverhampton Road works in 1925.

October 1926 saw its arrival at the Tilbury Docks project where it saw action until February 1929 before moving to Southampton. There, it was engaged in the building of the New (Western) Docks for two years until removed to McAlpine's Great Stanney and Hayes depots, after which it appeared at the Mogden Sewage works in December 1933. Having stayed there until January 1935, it returned briefly to Hayes, before dispatch to the Cheddar Reservoir the following month.

Ebbw Vale was the next location from October 1936 until December 1937, when yet another move took it to Bridgend. Six months later a spell at Appleby Frodingham Steel Co, Scunthorpe beckoned, before a final return to Hayes in July 1937 where it remained until sold to John Mowlem & Co for work on their contract at ROF Swynnerton, in December 1939. At this location, it was named *Staines*, and it remained so when moved to another Mowlem contract at the Llanberis Air Ministry Depot, where it was renumbered WD69 in 1941, and subsequently WD70069. By 1942, it was at the Central Ordnance Depot, Bicester, and then at Crewe North Shed by July 1945.

It was eventually sold by the Ministry of Supply in March 1946, and after a rebuild by makers HC in 1947, it became the property of the National Coal Board at Boldon Colliery in February 1948, seeing out its time there until scrapped in 1959.

No 42 in Middlesex at the Mogden Sewage Works in 1934. (J.E. Simpson)

McAlpine Contract Locomotive 0-6-0ST Hudswell Clarke No 1529

Name:	*Sir Robert McAlpine & Sons No 44*
Manufacturer:	Hudswell Clarke & Co Ltd, Leeds
Works number:	1529
Built:	1924
Running number:	44
Cylinders:	13in x 20in
Driving wheels:	3ft 3½in
Wheelbase:	11ft 6in
Weight:	24ton 15cwt
At the docks:	1929-1931

No 44 arrived new to Sir Robert McAlpine & Sons when delivered to their Watford Bypass construction site in June 1924. After that project was completed in 1926, there followed a visit to Ellesmere Port and then Tilbury Docks in October that same year. On leaving Tilbury in June 1928, its next job was at the New (Western) Docks where work was already well under way by the time it arrived in 1929.

By early 1931, it was at McAlpine's Great Stanney depot before moving to Stanlow Oil Dock in March that year, where it remained until the following year. It then spent the next three years back at Great Stanney before its next engagement at the Cheddar Reservoir, which ended in October 1935. After that, it was immediately dispatched to the GKB steel works in Cardiff until April 1936, when it moved on to the Hollowell Reservoir in Northampton, until November 1937.

That same month brought a visit to the Appleby Frodingham Steel Co, Scunthorpe until June 1939, when it was sent to McAlpine's Hayes depot. The following December, it was sold to John Mowlem & Co, and used on their contract at the ROF Swynnerton, where it was given the name *Yeovil.* Thereafter, it was recorded en route to Mowlem's contract at the Llanberis Air Ministry Depot in July 1941, where it took the number WD68 and later WD70068. In 1942, it was transferred to either Faslane or Cairnryan before being loaned by the War Department to Slough Estates during 1944-5. By September 1945, it had arrived at WD Bordon as its final posting before being sold to the Steel Breaking & Dismantling Co at Chesterfield in April 1946. There it was scrapped a year later.

No 44 wearing a spark arrester at Stanlow Oil Dock in 1932. (H.W. Robinson)

McAlpine Contract Locomotive 0-6-0ST Hudswell Clarke No 1539

Name:	*Sir Robert McAlpine & Sons No 46*
Manufacturer:	Hudswell Clarke & Co Ltd, Leeds
Works number:	1539
Built:	1924
Running number:	46
Cylinders:	13in x 20in
Driving wheels:	3ft 3½in
Wheelbase:	11ft 6in
Working Pressure:	160psi
Tank capacity:	600gal
Weight:	24ton 15cwt
At the docks:	1929-1933

No 46 was supplied new to Sir Robert McAlpine & Sons at Bushey & Oxley Junction near Watford in July 1924, where it saw employment on the Watford Bypass between 1924 and 1926. Then came a move to Tilbury Docks in July 1926, where it remained until September 1928, subsequently arriving at Southampton in January 1929.

It was engaged in the construction of the New (Western) Docks for four years until there came a transfer to the Cheddar Reservoir in 1933. There, it was gainfully employed until September 1935 saw its dispatch to the GKB Steelworks in Cardiff, and the Welsh sojourn continued with a move to Ebbw Vale in 1936, before removal to the Hayes Depot in August 1938. After a laying up for over a year, it was eventually sold to John Mowlem & Co in December 1939 (as were others of the McAlpine stable) for use at their Royal Ordnance Factory contract at Swynnerton, where it was given the name *Hayle*. By 1941, it had been transferred to another ROF contract at Ruddington in Nottingham, then, after further use on the Workington breakwater contract, *Hayle* was laid up at Mowlem's yard in Hatfield, until sold to the Ministry of Agriculture, Wissington in 1944.

In May 1947, this locomotive was overhauled at the LNER Doncaster works before dispatch to the British Sugar Corporation at Wissington in June of that year. When that railway closed, *Hayle* was sold to Thomas W. Ward Ltd in July 1957. They, in turn, resold the loco to contractors Derek Crouch, who were engaged as a subcontractor at the Widdrington NCB open cast site, Northumberland in 1958. There, it acquired the new owner's name.

By 1969, *Derek Crouch* had been transferred to Crouch's depot at Eye, near Peterborough, where it was held in store and procured for preservation by the Peterborough Locomotive Society in June 1972. It was afterwards moved to the Nene Valley Railway, Wansford, and by April 1974, had worked the railway's first train. The locomotive was out of use by 1982, and is currently in storage on the NVR awaiting restoration.

HC No 1539 as "Derek Crouch" revels in preservation at Wansford during the Nene Valley Railway's early days. (Author's Collection)

McAlpine Contract Locomotive 0-6-0ST Hudswell Clarke No 1494

Name:	*Sir Robert McAlpine & Sons No 47*
Manufacturer:	Hudswell Clarke & Co Ltd, Leeds
Works number:	1494
Built:	1923
Running number:	47 (56 from 1932)
Cylinders:	12in x 18in
Driving wheels:	3ft 1in
Wheelbase:	10ft 6in
Weight:	21ton 10cwt
At the docks:	1929-1931

This locomotive was supplied new in 1923 to Sir W.G. Armstrong Whitworth & Co during their contract for demolition of the Chevet Tunnel near Wakefield, before being sold to Sir Robert McAlpine and Sons, and arriving at their Great Stanney Depot in October 1926. From that time, it worked on a contract at Tilbury Docks (with a brief spell on the Manchester Ship Canal at Ellesmere Port during 1927) until transfer to Southampton to work on the New (Western) Docks in April 1929.

On leaving in 1931, No 47 spent five years based at the Great Stanney and Hayes depots, where it was renumbered 56 in 1932 before employment at Hollowell Reservoir, Northants (1936-7), and Scunthorpe (1937-8), after which it returned to Hayes until 1941 when sent to the Royal Ordnance Factory at Burghfield for a year. It was then on hire to the Beds, Cambs & Hunts Electricity Company for a short spell in 1942, before moving to Yardley Chase, Northants until October that year. A spell of inactivity at the Hayes depot followed, until it was hired out to the Southern Gas Board at Reading during 1951. After returning to Hayes that same year, it remained idle until sold to Roe Brothers for scrap in February 1958.

McAlpine No 56 at Hayes in its final days on 9th February 1957. (53A Models of Hull Collection)

McAlpine Contract Locomotive 0-6-0ST Hudswell Clarke No 1510

Name:	*Sir Robert McAlpine & Sons No 48*
Manufacturer:	Hudswell Clarke & Co Ltd, Leeds
Works number:	1510
Built:	1923
Running number:	48
Cylinders:	12in x 18in
Driving wheels:	3ft 1in
Wheelbase:	10ft 6in
Weight:	21ton 10cwt
At the docks:	1929-1935

This loco began life when supplied to Sir W.G. Armstrong Whitworth & Co, for work on demolishing the LMS Chevet Tunnel near Wakefield (see also McAlpine No 47). It then joined Sir Robert McAlpine & Sons' fleet at Great Stanney in October 1926 as their No 48, and was immediately transferred to their contract at Tilbury Docks, where it remained until moving to Southampton Docks in May 1929. In 1931, it was sent back to makers Hudswell Clarke for repairs, returning to the docks in June that same year.

Being one of the last McAlpine locos to leave Southampton, it was sent to the Hayes depot in October 1935. The following year it was dispatched to Ebbw Vale in April, and from there, to the Cheddar Reservoir in May. The next move came in September 1937, this time for three months work at the Appleby Frodingham Steel Co, Scunthorpe, before returning to Hayes. However, by February 1938, it was back at Scunthorpe again, this time until June 1939, when it made its final trip back to Hayes before being sold to the engineering firm of Abelson & Co in December that year.

From there it passed to the War Department tramway at Shoeburyness, where it carried the numbers 9, then WD71677, and finally 011, before being sent for scrap at Thomas W. Ward in April 1959. There, it languished for several months before finally being broken up.

Hudswell Clarke No 1510 at Thomas W. Ward, Grays in October 1959. (J.P. Mullett)

McAlpine Contract Locomotive 0-6-0ST Hudswell Clarke No 1511

Name:	*Sir Robert McAlpine & Sons No 49*
Manufacturer:	Hudswell Clarke & Co Ltd, Leeds
Works number:	1511
Built:	1923
Running number:	49 (47 from 1933)
Cylinders:	12in x 18in
Driving wheels:	3ft 1in
Wheelbase:	10ft 6in
Weight:	21ton 10cwt
At the docks:	1931-1933

This locomotive began life when supplied to Sir W.G. Armstrong Whitworth & Co. for work on demolishing the LMS Chevet Tunnel near Wakefield. It then joined Sir Robert McAlpine & Sons' fleet as No 49 at their Tilbury Docks contract in October 1926. It remained there until August 1929, before moving to McAlpine's Great Stanney depot, where it stayed for two years before being sent back to the makers for repairs in 1931.

After these works were completed in August that year, it became employed by McAlpine on the building of the New (Western) Docks, until going back to Great Stanney in 1933. From there it went to the Hayes depot, where it was renumbered 47 and moved to Mogden Sewage works in November 1933. It stayed there until transferred back to Hayes in 1935, when it was hired out to the local Gramophone Company, but before the year was out, it had ventured north to the Birkenhead Southern Outfall sewer, where the following year saw a return to Great Stanney.

After four years of inactivity, it was sold to another branch of the family firm, Alfred McAlpine in May 1950, but having moved to their Ellesmere Port depot it appears to have had little further employment before being scrapped in 1964.

McAlpine Contract Locomotive 0-6-0ST Manning Wardle No 1560

Name:	*Sir Robert McAlpine & Sons No 53*
Manufacturer:	Manning Wardle & Co Ltd, Hunslet, Leeds
Works number:	1560
Built:	1902
Running number:	53
Cylinders:	12in x 18in
Driving wheels:	3ft 0in
Wheelbase:	10ft 9in
Weight:	19ton 10cwt
At the docks:	1929-1934

This Manning Wardle locomotive was supplied new to contractors Mitchell Brothers as their No 7 in June 1902, for use during the construction of the Cairn Valley Light Railway, Dumfries, before being sold to the firm of H. Lovatt in 1905, where it was renumbered 20 and took the name *Catterall*. It was later renumbered 5 when engaged on the GWR Ealing to Shepherds Bush Railway in 1915. After that, Lovatt's transferred it to their contract at the Ministry of Munitions at Queensferry, where it became MoM property, and was also possibly used at British Dyes in Huddersfield.

It had come under the ownership of George Cohen and Armstrong by the time it was sold to Sir Robert McAlpine & Sons in October 1926, and taken to their Great Stanney depot. In July the following year, it was dispatched to their contract at Tilbury Docks where it was employed until August 1929. By October that year, it had found its way to Southampton until sent to McAlpine's Hayes depot in 1934. There followed trips to the Hollowell Reservoir, Northampton in August 1936 and the Appleby Frodingham Steel Co, Scunthorpe in July 1938, before the loco was broken up in 1939.

McAlpine Contract Locomotive 0-4-0ST Hudswell Clarke No 1537

Name:	*Sir Robert McAlpine & Sons No 52*
Manufacturer:	Hudswell Clarke & Co Ltd, Leeds
Works number:	1537
Built:	1924
Running number:	52
Cylinders:	9in x 15in
Driving wheels:	2ft 6½in
Wheelbase:	5ft 0in
Weight:	12ton 10cwt
At the docks:	1928-1929

No 52 arrived new to Sir Robert McAlpine & Sons at Ellesmere Port in July 1924 to work on the LMS sidings there. The following year, it was dispatched to the Bolton Corporation site at Crompton Way, before making its way to Tilbury Docks in September 1926. There it remained until March 1927, and in that same year it was employed on the Birmingham to Wolverhampton road construction before returning to Tilbury in October 1927 via a call at the company's Great Stanney depot. Employment at Tilbury lasted until October 1928, when it was sent to Southampton Docks, this engagement lasting for just over a year until leaving for Great Stanney in November 1929.

Its next engagement was on the Otterspool Sea Wall during 1930-31, after which there were several years of inactivity at both Great Stanney and Hayes depots from October 1931 until August 1936. Further employment began with a trip to the Port of London's Royal Victoria Docks extension in September 1936, which lasted until June the following year, when it was sent to Ebbw Vale for four months. Leaving there for Hayes in October the same year heralded another idle period, until it was sent to the RAF at Harpur Hill, Buxton in June 1939.

By May 1940, it was back at Hayes for another two years, after which it was transferred to Pauling & Co in March 1942 for use on the Magnesium Elektron contract at Lowerhouse, Burnley, where it carried the number 293. The following year, it was at the former Crymlyn Burrows, Swansea depot of Topham, Jones & Railton before being finally sold to George Brothers for scrap in 1951.

No 52 at Hayes on 18th December 1937 sporting a very modest cab. (G. Alliez)

McAlpine Contract Locomotive 0-6-0ST Hudswell Clarke No 1601

Name:	*Sir Robert McAlpine & Sons No 54*
Manufacturer:	Hudswell Clarke & Co Ltd, Leeds
Works number:	1601
Built:	1927
Running number:	54
Cylinders:	12in x 18in
Driving wheels:	3ft 1½in
Wheelbase:	10ft 6in
Weight:	21ton 10cwt
At the docks:	1931–1933

This locomotive was supplied direct from the makers to Sir Robert McAlpine & Sons' contract at Tilbury Docks in July 1927, where it worked until moved to their Great Stanney depot in February 1929. In December that year, it was dispatched to Bowater's Paper Mill at Ellesmere Port, spending exactly a year there before returning to Great Stanney. The move to Southampton came in October 1931, and following its time there, was sent back to Great Stanney by November 1933, and almost immediately moved to the company's other depot at Hayes.

A month later, it was at Mogden Sewage Works, where it was employed until February 1935, when it was sent to Hardingstone Power station, Northampton after a few days at the Hayes depot. From there came a transfer to Ebbw Vale in April 1936 until September 1938, after which it was back to Hayes again, and from there it was sent to the makers for repairs in January 1940.

Returning from a rebuild at Hudswell Clarke, it was sent directly to the Earley Power station in April 1941, where it stayed until June 1947. After another fifteen months of idleness at Hayes, it moved on again to a contract for British Railways at Grantshouse in September 1948, remaining there until November that year. Then came a final stay at Hayes, where it remained idle until it was sold to Roe Brothers for scrap in July 1956.

A weather-beaten No 54 languishes at Hayes on 29th October 1955. (G. Alliez)

McAlpine Contract Locomotive 0-6-0ST Hudswell Clarke No 1585

Name:	*Sir Robert McAlpine & Sons No 55*
Manufacturer:	Hudswell Clarke & Co Ltd, Leeds
Works number:	1585
Built:	1927
Running number:	55
Cylinders:	13in x 20in
Driving wheels:	3ft 3½in
Wheelbase:	11ft 6in
Working pressure:	160psi
Tank capacity:	600gal
Weight:	24ton 15cwt
At the docks:	1929-1932

Having been dispatched by the makers directly to Sir Robert McAlpine & Sons' contract at Tilbury Docks in July 1927, No 55 worked there until transferred to Southampton in April 1929. There, it spent three years on site before going off to the company's Great Stanney depot in April 1932. Its next call was in November 1934 to the Cheddar Reservoir, where it stayed until October 1936 when sent to McAlpine's other depot at Hayes.

Around this time, it was rebuilt at Hudswell Clarke, and was not seen again until appearing at Ebbw Vale, where it remained until March 1938. In May that year, it was moved to the Royal Ordnance Factory at Bridgend before returning to Hayes in May 1940. By June, it was on hire to the RAOC at Thatcham for three months, before moving to the Royal Ordnance Factory at Burghfield in February 1941 where its stay lasted until October that year. The period from November 1941 to March 1942 was spent at Renfrew before immediate dispatch to ICI Girvan until December that year. Then it moved on yet again to opencast workings at Ashby-de-la-Zouch, where it remained until further travels to Boscombe Down from February 1944 until July that year.

It was then stored at the Hayes depot until December of that year when it was sent to Hams Hall power station. There, it worked until September 1947, and was later transferred to Nechells Power Station in July 1948 for just 13 days. That month, it returned to the Hayes Depot until December 1948, when its presence was required at the Croydon "B" power station for two years. On its return to Hayes in December 1949, No 55 remained in the yard until sold to Roe Brothers for scrap in March 1958.

A woodland setting for No 55 engaged at the Croydon "B" Power Station contract on 11th February 1949. (G. Alliez)

McAlpine Contract Locomotive 0-6-0ST Hudswell Clarke No 1602

Name:	*Sir Robert McAlpine & Sons No 56*
Manufacturer:	Hudswell Clarke & Co Ltd, Leeds
Works number:	1602
Built:	1927
Running number:	56 (87A from 1940)
Cylinders:	12in x 18in
Driving wheels:	3ft 1½in
Wheelbase:	10ft 6in
Weight:	21ton 10cwt
At the docks:	1932-1934

No 56 was supplied new to Sir Robert McAlpine & Sons in August 1927, and sent directly to work at their Tilbury Docks contract, where it remained until moving to the Wimbledon-Sutton Railway in January 1929. Spells at Romford (widening the LNER line in 1930-1) and at Irlam Wharf on the Manchester Ship Canal (1931-2) followed before arrival at Southampton in March 1932.

On leaving the docks in June 1934, No 56 headed west to the GKB contract at Cardiff (1934-6) and then on to Ebbw Vale (1936) before working on the Cheddar Reservoir (1936-7). It then moved to the Appleby-Frodingham Steel Co, Scunthorpe (1937-8) before being hired out to George Wimpey & Co at Park Royal for four months at the end of 1938. During the following year, this much-travelled loco was hired out to The Gramophone Co at Hayes for six months in 1939, before another visit to Wimpey over the festive period of 1939-40. In 1940, the loco was renumbered No 87A by McAlpine and, from March, it spent over a year at Dalbeattie before returning to Hayes in April 1941, where it remained until November that year.

From there it was sent to the Cheltenham to Gloucester widening contract between November 1941 and July 1942, before returning to Hayes where it was stored until January 1945. It then took up duties at the Hams Hall power station, a stint lasting until June 1947, after which it was transferred to Dunston Power Station for two months. Back at Hayes in August 1947 it languished unused for 10 years until it was sent to Roe Brothers for scrap in November 1957.

McAlpine No 56 pictured at Sutton on 15th June 1929. (R.A. Wheeler)

McAlpine Contract Locomotive 0-6-0ST Hudswell Clarke No 1586

Name:	*Sir Robert McAlpine & Sons No 57*
Manufacturer:	Hudswell Clarke & Co Ltd, Leeds
Works number:	1586
Built:	1927
Running number:	57 (45 from 1933)
Cylinders:	13in x 20in
Driving wheels:	3ft 3½in
Wheelbase:	11ft 6in
Working pressure:	160psi
Tank capacity:	600gal
Weight:	24ton 15cwt
At the docks:	1929-1933

Hudswell Clarke No 1586 was supplied new to Sir Robert McAlpine & Sons as their No 57, and sent directly to work at Tilbury Docks in August 1927, where it remained until December 1928 before moving to Southampton in January 1929 for a four year stay until August 1933. Renumbered 45, it then moved on to the Cheddar Reservoir until a further deployment at Ebbw Vale began in May 1936. That lasted until March 1938, when it was transferred to the Royal Ordnance Factory at Bridgend, its time there ending in June 1939 with a move to McAlpine's depot at Hayes in Middlesex.

Clayton-le-Moors was the next port of call from November 1939 until April 1940, when a move to Dalbeattie lasted almost a year before transfer back to Hayes in May 1941. The Cheltenham to Gloucester widening scheme was next to play host to this locomotive in October 1941, where alternate duties at Yardley Chase, Northampton, kept it occupied until April 1943, when once again it found its way back to Hayes.

No further activity was recorded until April 1950, when a three-year stint at Keadby Power Station proved to be its last assignment. After a final return to Hayes in March 1953 it remained idle until sold to Roe Brothers for scrap in May 1958.

Note: McAlpine locomotives Nos 57 and 45 swapped numbers in 1933, and although both locos worked at Southampton, they were there at different times.

By now renumbered 45, Hudswell Clarke No 1586 rests at Hayes on 18th February 1939. (G. Alliez)

Western Docks – Brand 1929-1931

Contractors Charles Brand & Son were engaged during McAlpine's building of the New (Western) Docks, and their principal task was the construction of drains and culverts around the new works. They employed their own loco, a Barclay 0-4-0ST.

Brand Contract Locomotive 0-4-0ST Andrew Barclay No 747

Manufacturer:	Andrew Barclay & Sons Ltd, Kilmarnock
Works number:	747
Built:	1894
Cylinders:	12in x 20in
Driving wheels:	3ft 2in
Wheelbase:	5ft 6in
At the docks:	1929–1931

Andrew Barclay No 747 was supplied new to Charles Brand & Son in August 1894, and initially employed on the Inverness to Culdoich line being constructed for the Highland Railway. By February 1899, it had moved to another contract, this time for the construction of Grangemouth Docks. By November 1916, it had arrived at the extension works at Clunie Harbour before moving on to the Northburn Steelworks contract by May the following year. It was next recorded at another contract for the London underground in Golders Green by September 1922.

This locomotive then went on hire to contractors Stewart & Partners, who were engaged in the construction of the Twyford Bypass (from 1920 until 1926). Upon completion, it was returned to owners Charles Brand, and subsequently worked on the construction drains and culverts at Southampton's New Docks (now Western Docks). This appointment lasted from 1929 until 1931, the work being carried out under the main contractor Sir Robert McAlpine.

After leaving Southampton, the locomotive was taken to Brand's plant depot at Tooting in London, and from there, it found its way to the Fulham Gasworks, via George Cohen, before being sold to the firm of Rowland Clark in October 1954. By April 1955, it was working at the Thurrock Chalk & Whiting Co Ltd at Essex (where it was named *Planet*) until its end came when sold to Thomas W. Ward for scrap in March 1966.

Brand's Andrew Barclay No 747 at work on the London Underground line between Colindale and Edgware in 1922. (F. Jones Collection)

King George V Graving Dock – Mowlem 1931-1935

As if the enormity of the Western Dock construction was not enough, in the midst of it all the Southern Railway set about building what was then the world's largest dry dock (No 7) named the King George V Graving Dock. Work on this was carried out simultaneously with the New Docks venture from 1931 to 1935. The joint contractors were John Mowlem & Co and Edmund Nuttall & Sons, but it would appear that all the eighteen locos used were owned by Mowlem.

The Graving Dock was officially opened on 26th July 1933, appropriately by the King himself. Its construction called for the excavation of two million tons of earth and some 750,000 tons of concrete were used. At 1,200 feet long and over 100 feet wide it needed four 1250hp, 54-inch diameter pumps to drain it. To accommodate the huge workforce employed by the various ship repairing firms, a canteen and waiting room capable of holding 1200 men was provided.

A Mowlem loco works in the base of the growing dry dock in 1932. (Associated British Ports)

The giant dry dock takes shape inside the protective earth works. (Author's Collection)

RMS Queen Mary inches into the completed dry dock as the New Docks quayside and sheds stretch out in the background. (Author's Collection)

Mowlem Contract Locomotive 0-4-0ST L&YR No 1097

Name:	*Bassett*
Manufacturer:	Lancashire & Yorkshire Railway, Horwich
Works number:	1097
Built:	1910
Running numbers:	19 (L&Y), 11243 (LMS)
Cylinders:	13in x 18in
Driving wheels:	3ft ½in
Working pressure:	160psi
Weight:	21ton 5 cwt
At the docks:	1931-1935

One of a class of locos known as "Pugs" that was introduced by the L&Y in 1891 for dock shunting. Several were sold off by the LMS in the 1930s, this example going to John Mowlem in September 1931 for work on construction of the King George V Graving Dock. On completion of the project, it was sold on to the United Glass Bottle Manufacturers at Charlton in 1935, where it was renamed *Prince*.

In January 1967, at the end of its time there, this locomotive (by now unnamed) was handed over to the Railway Preservation Society at Quainton Road, and stored at Luton until transferred to the Keighley & Worth Valley Railway in October 1969. With the cost of returning it to working order being prohibitive, it was restored as a static exhibit, and is now at the Ribble Steam Railway awaiting public display.

Former L&Y Pug "Bassett" proudly carries its new name for Mowlem at Southampton Docks on 25th September 1932. (H.F. Wheeller / R.S. Carpenter Collection)

Mowlem Contract Locomotive 0-6-0ST Avonside No 1894

Name:	*Blythe*
Manufacturer:	Avonside Engine Co Ltd, Bristol
Works number:	1894
Built:	1922
Cylinders:	14½in x 20in
Driving wheels:	3ft 3in
Wheelbase:	9ft 8½in
At the docks:	1931-1935

Blythe was supplied new to the Nidd Valley Light Railway for Bradford Corporation Waterworks, and worked there until purchase by Mowlem and its arrival at Southampton in 1931. After leaving the docks it was sold to dealers Joseph Pugsley & Sons Ltd, at Stoke Gifford in Gloucester in 1936, before being resold to the Amalgamated Denaby Collieries at Rossington Main Colliery in the same year. Then, in January 1947, on the Nationalisation of the coal industry, it came under the ownership of the National Coal Board at Doncaster, where it was eventually scrapped at Rossington in 1968.

Mowlem Contract Locomotive 0-4-0ST Hawthorn Leslie No 3760

Name:	*Beaulieu*
Manufacturer:	R. & W. Hawthorn Leslie & Co, Newcastle-on-Tyne
Works number:	3760
Built:	1932
Cylinders:	12in x 20in
Driving wheels:	3ft 1in
At the docks:	1932-1933

Beaulieu arrived new to John Mowlem & Co at Southampton Docks in February 1932 when it was delivered to them for work on King George V Graving Dock. In 1933, it was sold to the Thurrock Chalk & Whiting Co Ltd in Essex where, renamed *P.H.B*, it worked on until sent to Thomas W. Ward at Grays for scrap in March 1966.

Mowlem Contract Locomotive 0-6-0ST HC No 1593

Name:	*Bobby*
Manufacturer:	Hudswell Clarke & Co, Leeds
Works number:	1593
Built:	1927
Cylinders:	14in x 20in
Driving wheels:	3ft 7in
Wheelbase:	10ft 3in
Weight:	29ton 10cwt
At the docks:	1931-1935

This locomotive was supplied new to George Armitage & Sons at Robin Hood in Yorkshire, where *Bobby* was employed until sold to John Mowlem & Co Ltd in 1931, having being overhauled by the makers prior to its arrival at Southampton Docks.

After completion of the King George V Graving Dock project in 1935, the locomotive was moved in 1936 to another Mowlem contract at Chingford Reservoir in Essex, where it took the name *London John*. In 1944, it was on hire to the Blaenavon contract for the Ministry of Fuel & Power, and in the following year, it was working at West Hallam Disposal Point in Derbyshire. By 1947, it had been loaned to Samuel Williams & Sons at Dagenham Dock, before returning to its owners in February 1950. It was then loaned to the Thorpe Brickworks of George Armitage & Sons at Ardley in Yorkshire before undergoing an overhaul at the works of makers Hudswell Clarke. The loco ended its days at Mowlem's Marshmoor works, near Hatfield, and was sold for scrap to J.W. Hardwick Sons & Co at West Ewell in April 1963.

Mowlem Contract Locomotive 0-6-0ST Hunslet No 1690

Name:	*Cunarder*
Manufacturer:	Hunslet Engine Co Ltd, Hunslet, Leeds
Works number:	1690
Built:	1931
Cylinders:	14in x 20in
Driving wheels:	3ft 4in
Wheelbase:	9ft 0in
Weight:	30ton 5cwt
At the docks:	1931-1935

This engine arrived new to John Mowlem & Co Ltd in July 1931 and went straight to the construction of the King George V Graving Dock. On completion, *Cunarder* was transferred to fellow contractor Edmund Nuttall & Sons' ownership, and taken to their sea wall contract at Wallasey, Cheshire in 1935. It was later engaged in works at the Royal Ordnance Factories at Glascoed and Hirwaun between 1939 and 1942, and subsequently at the Cliff Quay Power Station at Ipswich in 1945.

During 1945 it was on loan to Samuel Williams & Sons at Dagenham Dock, but returned to Nuttall in September that year. Another visit to Williams took place between November 1954 and March 1955, and by March 1957 it had been sold to APCM (latterly Blue Circle) at Harbury Works, in Warwickshire, where it remained in service until transferred to the Railway Preservation Society at Quainton Road in April 1969, as the property of the Cunarder Group.

Since then the locomotive has moved to the Swanage Railway where it ran in 1981, following restoration to its original form, but since then it has been rebuilt as an 0-6-0T, and is now undergoing another refurbishment by the 1708 Locomotive Preservation Trust at a private location.

Mowlem's loco "Beaulieu" stands alongside the contractor's on-site running shed at Southampton on 25th September 1932. (H.F. Wheeller / R.S. Carpenter Collection)

A forlorn "Bobby" lingers at Mowlem's Welham Green Depot. (J.K. Williams)

Hunslet 1690 "Cunarder" at APCM Harbury in September 1958. (P. D. Rowbotham)

Mowlem Contract Locomotive 0-6-0ST Hunslet No 1687

Name:	*Grosvenor*
Manufacturer:	Hunslet Engine Co Ltd, Hunslet, Leeds
Works number:	1687
Built:	1931
Cylinders:	14in x 20in
Driving wheels:	3ft 4in
Wheelbase:	9ft 0in
Weight:	30ton 5cwt
At the docks:	1931-1935

Grosvenor arrived new from the makers to John Mowlem & Co Ltd at Southampton Docks in July 1931. After completion of the King George V Graving Docks works, *Grosvenor* was transferred to the William Jones contract at Cantley, Norfolk in 1935. It was transferred to the British Sugar Corporation Cantley by 1941, and was finally scrapped by A. King & Son of Norwich in 1958.

Mowlem Contract Locomotive 0-4-0ST Avonside No 2037

Name:	*Itchen*
Manufacturer:	Avonside Engine Co Ltd, Bristol 1931
Works number:	2037
Built:	1931
Cylinders:	12in x 20in
Driving wheels:	3ft 1in
Wheelbase:	5ft 0in
Weight:	23ton 0cwt
At the docks:	1931-1934

Like many of its sisters, *Itchen* was delivered new to John Mowlem & Co Ltd at Southampton Docks for construction of the King George V Graving Dock. On completion of the works, it was taken to another Mowlem Southern Railway contract at the Dover Ferry Terminal in 1934. By 1939, it had moved to a different Mowlem site at ROF Swynnerton and by 1943, it was employed in the construction of Chingford No 2 Reservoir, where it took the name *Chingford*.

From there it was taken back to Mowlem's Welham Green Depot at Hatfield, Herts, where it remained until 1944, after which it was sent to the Metropolitan Water Board at Lea Bridge, returning once again to Mowlem in 1949, and eventually being scrapped there in 1956.

Some ad-hoc cab work and a severed front buffer signal the demise of "Itchen" at Mowlem's Welham Green Depot on 17th April 1954. (ILS Collection)

Mowlem Contract Locomotive 0-6-0ST Hunslet No 1648

Name:	*Millbrook*
Manufacturer:	Hunslet Engine Co Ltd, Hunslet, Leeds
Works number:	1648
Built:	1931
Cylinders:	14in x 20in
Driving wheels:	3ft 4in
Wheelbase:	9ft 0in
Weight:	30ton 5cwt
At the docks:	1931-1935

This locomotive arrived new at Southampton in May 1931 appropriately named after its initial workplace. After work at Southampton finished, *Millbrook* was engaged at the Chingford Reservoir contract. From there, this loco found itself in wartime service at the Temple Newsam Coal Disposal Plant at Leeds. This was operated by Sir Lindsay Parkinson & Co Ltd, until it was taken over by the Ministry of Fuel & Power from 1942. It would seem that *Millbrook* was back at the Chingford Reservoir by 1944, and remained there until February 1945. After a return to Mowlem's Welham Green Depot, it worked at their Shellhaven contract in Essex in 1949-50 and thereafter saw little activity until scrapped in 1956.

Hunslet No 1648 "Millbrook" pictured at Chingford on 16th May 1936. (B.D. Stoyel)

Mowlem Contract Locomotive 0-6-0ST Hunslet No 1685

Name:	*Nuttall*
Manufacturer:	Hunslet Engine Co Ltd, Hunslet, Leeds
Works number:	1685
Built:	1931
Cylinders:	14in x 20in
Driving wheels:	3ft 4in
Wheelbase:	9ft 0in
Weight:	30ton 5cwt
At the docks:	1931-1935

This locomotive was one of several new engines supplied to John Mowlem & Co Ltd, arriving at Southampton in July 1931, and was named in recognition of the project's joint contractors Edmund Nuttall, & Sons. When work at Southampton ended, it was transferred to Nuttall's ownership and taken to the company's contract at Wallasey, Cheshire where a new sea wall was being constructed.

That project ended in 1939, and the loco was subsequently engaged in works of the Royal Ordnance Factories at Glascoed, Hirwaun, and Elstow until 1942, when it was hired to the Ministry of Fuel & Power near Barnsley in September of that year. By 1944, it had joined former Southampton running mate *Mowlem* on loan to the Waterloo Main Colliery, near Leeds, and by September 1947 it had returned to Nuttall's depot at Colnbrook in Buckinghamshire.

In July 1948, it was back in Yorkshire when sold to the National Coal Board and transferred to the Walsall Wood Colliery. From there, it went to the Coppice Colliery from June 1950 to August 1955, and after a brief return to Walsall Wood, it was sent to Cannock Chase Central Workshops, Staffordshire in August 1956. Having spent the remainder of its life at several collieries in the West Midlands, it was scrapped at Lea Hall Colliery, Rugeley in August 1966.

Mowlem Contract Locomotive 0-6-0ST Hunslet No 1686

Name:	*Mowlem*
Manufacturer:	Hunslet Engine Co Ltd, Hunslet, Leeds
Works number:	1686
Built:	1931
Cylinders:	14in x 20in
Driving wheels:	3ft 4in
Wheelbase:	9ft 0in
Weight:	30ton 5cwt
At the docks:	1931-1935

Mowlem arrived at Southampton new from its makers in July 1931 having the distinction of bearing the name of the King George V Graving Dock project's main contractor. When that contract ended, *Mowlem* was transferred to fellow contractor, Edmund Nuttall & Son's ownership, and taken to that company's sea wall contract at Wallasey, Cheshire in 1935, where it was renamed *Wallasey*. Afterwards it was engaged on the Motspur Park to Chessington South line, which was constructed between 1937 and 1939, and further employment saw it at the Royal Ordinance Factories at Glascoed and Hirwaun in Glamorgan until June 1942.

Following a short spell at Nuttall's Colnbrook Depot in Buckinghamshire, it was hired to the Ministry of Fuel & Power at Temple Newsam near Leeds in August 1942. During 1943-4, it was on hire from Nuttall's to the Waterloo Main Colliery, near Leeds, and by September 1946 it had returned to Colnbrook. It remained there until at least 1953, and was hired to Samuel Williams at Dagenham in 1954-5 before returning to Nuttall's depot.

The loco was then sold to the Tunnel Portland Cement Co at West Thurrock in September 1959, where, two months later, it was joined by former Mowlem/Nuttall running mate *Southern*. The pair saw out the remainder of their working lives there until both were scrapped in April 1965.

Mowlem Contract Locomotive 0-6-0ST Manning Wardle No 1539

Name:	*Penn*
Manufacturer:	Manning Wardle & Co Ltd, Hunslet, Leeds
Works number:	1539
Built:	1902
Cylinders:	12in x 17in
Driving wheels:	3ft 0in
Wheelbase:	10ft 9in
Weight:	18ton 10cwt
At the docks:	1931-1935

Penn was originally supplied new to contractors Pauling & Co Ltd at Uxbridge in February 1902, and set to work on the Northolt Junction to High Wycombe line where construction ended in 1905. It was then employed at the Ebbw Vale Steel & Iron Co, and then wartime service saw it employed at Catterick army camp. Later, in 1921, it was used on the Ewden Reservoir construction for Sheffield Corporation Waterworks Department.

In 1930 it underwent an overhaul at the Yorkshire Engine Company, after which, in February 1931, it came to contractor John Mowlem & Co Ltd at Southampton (via George Cohen Sons & Co). After the docks contract was completed *Penn* went to Mowlem's Chingford Reservoir contract (again via Cohen in 1936), an assignment that lasted from 1937 until 1941. There is no further record after that engagement.

Hunslet 1686, ex-"Mowlem", at its final port of call in the store yard of the Tunnel Portland Cement Company's West Thurrock Depot on 28th October 1961. (J.K. Williams)

"Penn" pictured in Denham, Bucks in 1903. (S.W.A. Newton / Leicester Museum)

Mowlem Contract Locomotive 0-4-0ST Andrew Barclay No 1993

Name:	*Shirley*
Manufacturer:	Andrew Barclay & Sons Ltd, Kilmarnock
Works number:	1993
Built:	1932
Cylinders:	12in x 20in
Driving wheels:	3ft 2in
Wheelbase:	5ft 6in
At the docks:	1932-1934

Shirley arrived at Southampton new from the makers in April 1932. After completion of the King George V Graving Dock project, it was sent to Dover in 1934, where it worked on another Mowlem contract at the Train Ferry Terminal. It then became one of numerous locomotives employed by Mowlem during the construction of the Royal Ordnance Factory at Swynnerton in Staffordshire around 1940. By 1943, it had been sent to the Barking Generating Station at Creekmouth, Essex, before returning to Mowlem's Chingford depot in 1946. It was then dispatched to Brimsdown Generating Station in 1947 before returning to Welham Green the following year.

Shirley was then sent to the Chingford Reservoir before spending its latter years at Mowlem's Marshmoor Works near Hatfield, Herts, until sold to Pursers Engineering Co, Old Kent Road in October 1964, and thence to J.W. Hardwick Sons & Co for scrap in April 1965.

Mowlem Contract Locomotive 0-4-0ST Avonside No 2036

Name:	*Solent*
Manufacturer:	Avonside Engine Co Ltd, Bristol
Works number:	2036
Built:	1931
Cylinders:	12in x 20in
Driving wheels:	3ft 1in
Wheelbase:	5ft 0in
At the docks:	1931-1933

Solent arrived at Southampton new from the makers in 1931. In October 1933, it was sold to Bradley & Foster Ltd at Darlaston Green Furnaces in Staffordshire, and in 1946, it was loaned to G. & R. Thomas at Hatherton Furnaces, Bloxwich, Walsall, until returning to Bradley & Foster in 1948. It remained there until being scrapped in 1960.

Mowlem Contract Locomotive 0-6-0ST Hunslet No 1647

Name:	*Southampton*
Manufacturer:	Hunslet Engine Co Ltd, Hunslet, Leeds
Works number:	1647
Built:	1931
Cylinders:	14in x 20in
Driving wheels:	3ft 4in
Wheelbase:	9ft 0in
Weight:	30ton 5cwt
At the docks:	1931-1935

Southampton arrived at Southampton new from the makers in May 1931. After the King George V Graving Dock works were completed in 1935, it was transferred, via George Cohen & Sons, to another of Mowlem's contracts at Chingford Reservoir, Essex in 1936. In 1947, the locomotive was loaned to Samuel Williams & Sons at Dagenham Dock, until it was returned to Mowlem in February 1949. Another loan came in January 1953, to the Ford Motor Co Ltd at Dagenham, returning to Welham Green the following year, and being scrapped in 1955.

A neat looking "Shirley" parades at Mowlem's Welham Green Depot in 1957. (ILS Collection)

Mowlem Contract Locomotive 0-6-0ST Hunslet No 1688

Name:	*Southern*
Manufacturer:	Hunslet Engine Co Ltd, Hunslet, Leeds
Works number:	1688
Built:	1931
Cylinders:	14in x 20in
Driving wheels:	3ft 4in
Wheelbase:	9ft 0in
Weight:	30ton 5cwt
At the docks:	1931 - 1935

Southern arrived new from the makers in July 1931, and worked until completion of the King George V Graving Dock contract in 1935. It was then transferred to the ownership of fellow contractor Edmund Nuttall & Sons, who sent the locomotive, with sister engine *Mowlem*, to the company's sea wall contract at Wallasey, Cheshire in 1935.

Wartime duties saw *Southern* engaged in works at the Royal Ordnance Factories at Glascoed, Hirwaun and Pontrilas between 1939 and 1943, before moving on to the Cliff Quay Power Station at Ipswich in 1945. It was then on loan to the British Sugar Corporation at Ipswich from September 1945 until April 1946, after which it spent some years idle at Nuttall & Son's Colnbrook Depot, until being was sold to the Tunnel Portland Cement Co at West Thurrock in November 1959. Here, it was reunited again with *Mowlem* (now renamed *Wallasey*) while seeing out its final years there until being scrapped in April 1965.

Mowlem Contract Locomotive 0-6-0ST Avonside No 2001

Name:	*Test*
Manufacturer:	Avonside Engine Co Ltd, Bristol
Works number:	2001
Built:	1931
Cylinders:	14in x 22in
Driving wheels:	3ft 6in
Wheelbase:	9ft 8½in
At the docks:	1931-1934

Test arrived at Southampton from the makers in 1931, but as the King George V Graving Dock project neared its completion, the locomotive was sold (via dealers George Cohen Sons & Co) to Associated Portland Cement Manufacturers at their Bevans Works in Northfleet, Kent in July 1934. By this time, the loco had lost its name, and spent the remainder of its years in anonymity at APCM before being scrapped in March 1951.

Mowlem Contract Locomotive 0-6-0ST Hunslet No 1689

Name:	*Trafford Park*
Manufacturer:	Hunslet Engine Co Ltd, Hunslet, Leeds
Works number:	1689
Built:	1931
Cylinders:	14in x 20in
Driving wheels:	3ft 4in
Wheelbase:	9ft 0in
Weight:	30ton 5cwt
At the docks:	1931-1935

Trafford Park was delivered new to John Mowlem & Co at Southampton in July 1931. When the King George V Graving Dock project was completed in 1935, it passed through the hands of dealers George Cohen & Sons before being re-engaged by Mowlem at their Chingford Reservoir contract in 1936.

It was still with them in 1948, when it was sent on loan to Samuel Williams & Sons at Dagenham Dock, and after its return, it was loaned again in 1949, this time to the National Coal Board at Upper Portland Screens, Pinxton, Nottinghamshire. From there, still with the NCB, it moved to Alma Screens, North Wingfield, Derbyshire in July of that year, returning to Mowlem in December 1950. It was scrapped in 1956.

Mowlem Contract Locomotive 0-4-0ST Andrew Barclay No 1411

Name:	*Witham*
Manufacturer:	Andrew Barclay & Sons Ltd, Kilmarnock
Works number:	1411
Built:	1915
Cylinders:	12in x 20in
Driving wheels:	3ft 2in
Wheelbase:	5ft 6in
At the docks:	1931-1935

This loco was supplied new, bearing the name *Don*, to T. Firth & Sons, Sheffield, and was sold in July 1919 to Clayton & Shuttleworth at Stamp End, Lincoln, before moving to George Cohen's depot at Stanningly, Yorks in 1931. It arrived at Southampton docks in that same year where, carrying the name *Witham*, it was employed by John Mowlem & Co on the construction of the King George V Graving Dock. After the contract was completed in 1935, it was sold to British Portland Cement Manufacturers at Wouldham Works, West Thurrock in Essex, where it carried the owners running number 10, until it became one of eight steam locos scrapped by them in July 1961.

A battle-weary "Witham" rests between labours at BPCM's Wouldham Works on 27th March 1956. (ILS Collection)

Union Castle Quays – McAlpine 1939

Having completed the construction of the Western Docks some four years earlier, Sir Robert McAlpine & Sons were recalled to widen the Union Castle quayside along berths 34, 35 and 36 in the Eastern Docks. Two locomotives were engaged in the work, one of these, No 32, had been involved in the earlier contract, and it was joined by No 57 for this project. During the works, Union Castle switched their operations to 106 berth in the New (Western) Docks, until the modified quays were reopened in February 1940.

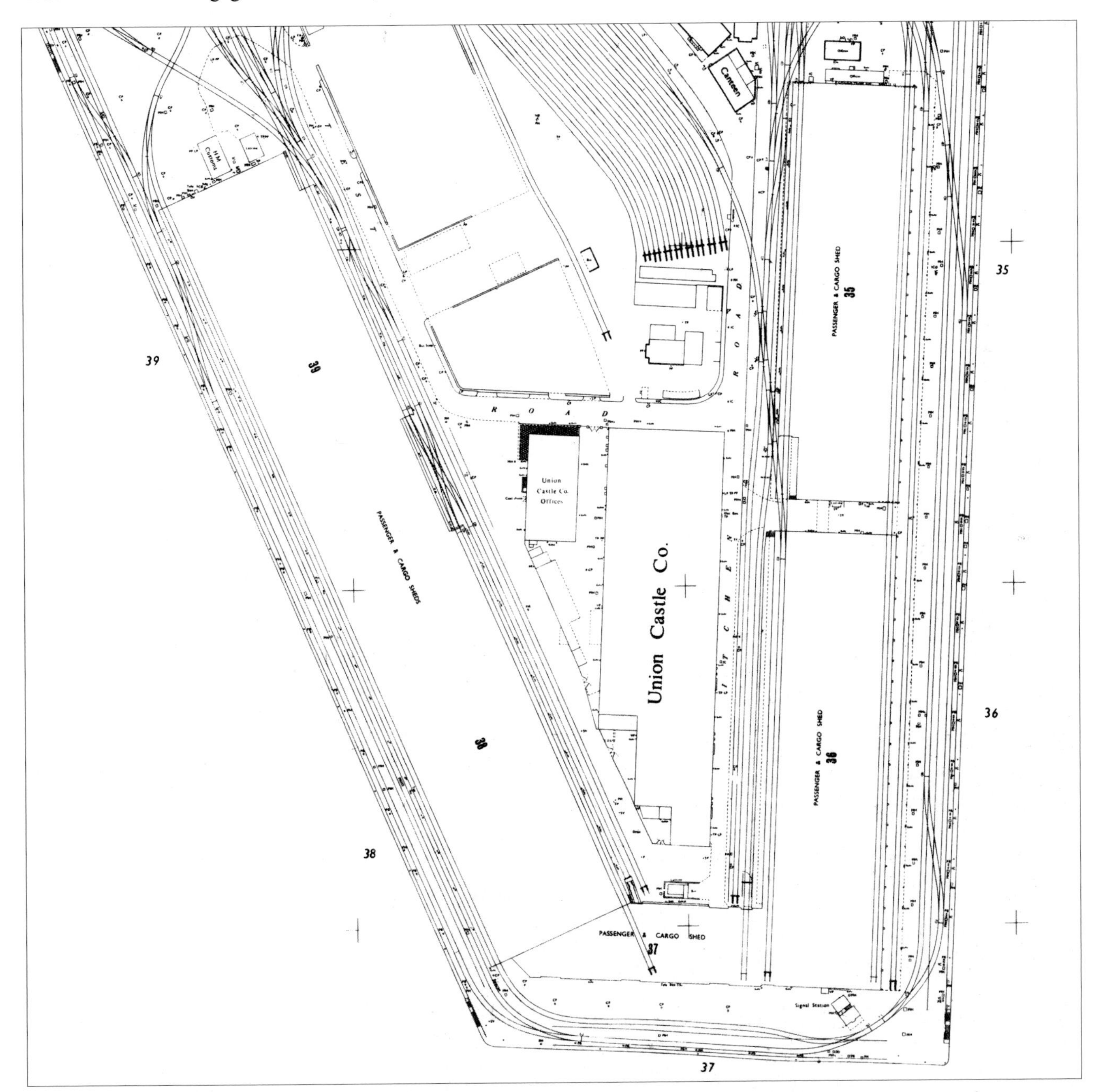

Union Castle Line's headquarters at the rear of berths 35/6 in the Eastern Docks after 1939.

McAlpine Contract Locomotive 0-6-0ST Hudswell Clarke No 1028

Name:	*Sir Robert McAlpine & Sons No 32*
Manufacturer:	Hudswell Clarke & Co Ltd, Leeds
Works number:	1028
Built:	1913
Running numbers:	32
At the docks:	1929–1931 and 1939

After an earlier engagement at Southampton, where it worked on the White Star Dock from in May 1929 until July 1931, No 32 returned to the docks in January 1939 as one of two locomotives employed by McAlpine during the widening of the Union Castle Line quays, after which it returned to the contractor's Hayes depot in December that year.

Full details of this locomotive appear in the McAlpine notes on the White Star Dock contract.

McAlpine Contract Locomotive 0-6-0ST Hudswell Clarke No 1538

Name:	*Sir Robert McAlpine & Sons No 45*
Manufacturer:	Hudswell Clarke & Co Ltd, Leeds
Works number:	1538
Built:	1924
Running numbers:	57 (No 45 until 1933)
Cylinders:	13in x 20in
Driving wheels:	3ft 3½in
Wheelbase:	11ft 6in
Weight:	24ton 15cwt
At the docks:	1939

Supplied new to Sir Robert McAlpine & Sons at Watford Junction in July 1924, this loco also worked on projects at the Watford Bypass (1924-26) after which was employed at Ellesmere Port on the Manchester Ship Canal, before moving on to Tilbury Docks from October 1926 until November 1928. Having been based at the company's Great Stanney Depot for two years afterwards, it found its way to Elderslie Dock in September 1931 for a year.

After another visit to Great Stanney, where it was renumbered No 57 in 1933, it was employed at Bowater's Mersey Wharf from December 1934 until May 1935. A brief stopover at the Cheddar Reservoir preceded further layoffs at Great Stanney and Hayes depots (1935-6) until it transferred to Hollowell Reservoir in Northampton (1936-7). Scunthorpe was its base in 1937, until it returned to Hayes in June 1938.

It arrived at Southampton in May 1939 for the widening of the Union Castle quays, its employment there lasting until October of that year, but for a period during June it was loaned to the docks Engineer's Department (see Chapter 5).

Its docks duties were followed by a return to the Hayes depot, from where it was sold to John Mowlem & Co, who employed it on their contract at the Royal Ordnance Factory at Swynnerton from November 1939. By 1942 it was languishing in the company depot at Welham Green and no further whereabouts were noted until it was sold to the British Sugar Corporation at South Lynn in 1944, finally being scrapped in 1963.

Note: McAlpine locomotives numbers 45 and 57 swapped numbers in 1933. Although both locos worked at Southampton, they were there at different times and on different projects.

CHAPTER 7

Town Quay Tramway 1847-1970

When the *Mayflower* sailed from Southampton in 1602, ships docked at the West Quay, and it wasn't until 1803 that the Harbour Commissioners were formed by Act of Parliament to improve quayside facilities. The Water Gate at the bottom of the High Street, and the clutter of ramshackle buildings around it, were cleared away, and the Town Quay area was redeveloped with improvements to the old stone jetty. By 1833, a new (Royal) Pier had been constructed – all this before any thought was given to building proper docks. That followed with the formation of the Southampton Dock Company some three years later, the foundation stone being laid in 1838.

The Town Quay and Royal Pier were administered quite separately from the docks by the Harbour Commissioners (subsequently the Harbour Board) who were responsible for port conservancy until being absorbed by the dock authority in 1968. While being mainly concerned with such matters as buoy maintenance, navigational aids, and channel dredging, the Board also provided warehousing and cranage for continental and coastwise vessels at the Town Quay.

Until the coming of the London and Southampton Railway (later the LSWR) in 1840, there was no form of public transport to the Pier and Quay. Barrowmen would convey passengers' effects to local hotels before they were transported onwards by stagecoach. With the close proximity of the main line railway, the Harbour Commissioners now sought to build a tramway to link its facilities with those at the Southampton Town (later Terminus) Station.

The Dock Company and the railway saw this as being against their interests, and combined their opposition to the application most vigorously, but eventually they were overruled, and by 1847 a tramway had been constructed from the Town Station to the Town Quay, this being leased to the LSWR from 1851.

Goods and passengers could now connect (almost) directly with the main line, but not quite, as the tramway rails terminated on the south side of the Canute Road and didn't actually meet those at the station on the other side of the street until a turntable connection was installed later. The tramway ran westwards from the Terminus Station along the northern perimeter of the Dock Company land, passing outside its main entrance (now Dock Gate 4) and along Platform Road until reaching the Quay at the bottom of the High Street, where several sidings were laid out.

The peaceful Town Quay railway scene looking landwards circa 1880. (Southampton City Archive)

Trees between the tramway tracks caused clearance problems at the Platform in 1895. (Southampton City Archive)

This 1908 photograph of B4 Class No 91 crossing Canute Road shows the two lines running towards the Town Quay and Royal Pier. The one on the right is the original tramway, while the other on the left is the later connection. (Southampton University Industrial Archaeology Group)

The service was horse-drawn, and as trade continued to grow, the Town Quay was extended seawards in 1853. The following decades saw further development and lengthening of the Quay, together with several warehouses being erected on the adjacent land. In 1870, the Commissioners decided to upgrade the tramway by eliminating various turntables, and at the same time, extending it further to the Royal Pier. By 1871, a direct connection had been established across Canute Road to the LSWR rails at the Terminus Station.

At this time the railway was still leasing the tramway, and by 1876, steam traction had been introduced on the Royal Pier service (see Chapter 8). The three locomotives employed there (*Southampton*, *Cowes* and *Ritzebuttel*) also performed shunting duties at the Town Quay, but by March 1901, former Dock Company engines *Bretwalda* and *Clausentum* had replaced *Ritzebuttel* and *Cowes*, and within a year, *Bretwalda* had moved on to the Bournemouth area.

Clausentum and *Southampton* worked the Quay traffic between them, until the latter was sent to Winchester in late 1906, motor tanks having taken over the Pier service. From that date *Clausentum* was retained for shunting work, although regularly relieved by class C14 No 744, and from September 1912 by ex-LBSCR "Terrier" No 734. From 1913, after 734 had been shipped to the Isle of Wight, the duties were often rotated with class C14 Nos 743 and 745, until *Clausentum* was eventually transferred to Guildford in March 1924, with former Southampton Dock Company partner *Ironside* moving in the opposite direction.

The C14 locomotives were successors to the ill-fated rail motors, being originally constructed as 2-2-0Ts with a trailing passenger coach. Unfortunately, they proved equally unsuccessful through lack of power, especially when an extra coach was required in peak times. However, in 1913, several were rebuilt as 0-4-0T locomotives, and this pair proved splendidly suitable to working the tight curves on the Town Quay. Their main dimensions were:

Cylinders:	10in x 14in (14in x 14in after conversion to 0-4-0T)
Driving wheels:	3ft 0in
Wheelbase:	8ft 0in

This view, taken around 1900, shows one of the former Dock Company locomotives at work on the Town Quay. (Southampton City Archive)

Working pressure: 150psi
Tank capacity: 500gal
Weight: 24ton 0cwt (later 25ton 15cwt)

Being operators of both the docks and the Pier railways, in 1912, the LSWR abandoned the tramway section between the Town Quay and Terminus Station, after diverting services through the docks estate. The area outside and west of the main Dock Gate was widened to provide sidings for the Town Quay freight traffic, and the disused tramway was eventually covered over, but part of the trackwork was rediscovered, still buried in the roadway, when new utility services were laid through the dock gate in the 1990s.

In November 1917, No 743 was sold to the Admiralty at Portsmouth, while 745 had maintained service on the Quay during World War I, until it was later joined by others of the class (Nos 741 and 744) in 1920. The trio rotated duties until October 1927, when 745 (by now renumbered 0745 by the Southern Railway) was transferred to departmental service and sent to Redbridge Sleeper Depot as No 77s.

0741 and 0744 (as they now were) continued working regularly at the Quay, and under further renumbering became 3741 and 3744, then finally 30588 and 30589 under British Railways. The two were eventually withdrawn from service in December 1957, following which, No 77s returned to its old haunts for a final spell of duty that lasted until being scrapped in April 1959.

After the demise of the C14s, duties at the Town Quay were carried out by Drewry diesel shunters based at the Terminus Station yard. By the late 1960s the mainstay of Quay traffic was Scandinavian timber, imported by Montague Meyer, but a revision of charges by BR forced Meyers to switch to road transport, and that was effectively the death knell for the rail borne freight service, which was finally discontinued in May 1970.

However, the Town Quay area still saw train movements for several more years as the docks traffic moved along the adjacent rails that linked the Eastern and Western Docks. This line passed by the old Harbour Board offices and Royal Pier entrance until, it too, was closed in October 1979.

During the 1990s the Town Quay warehouses and workshops were demolished, making way for a new commercial and retail development, since when only a few traces of the old railway remain.

C14 Class No 741 shunting at the Town Quay in the early 1920s. (H.C. Casserley)

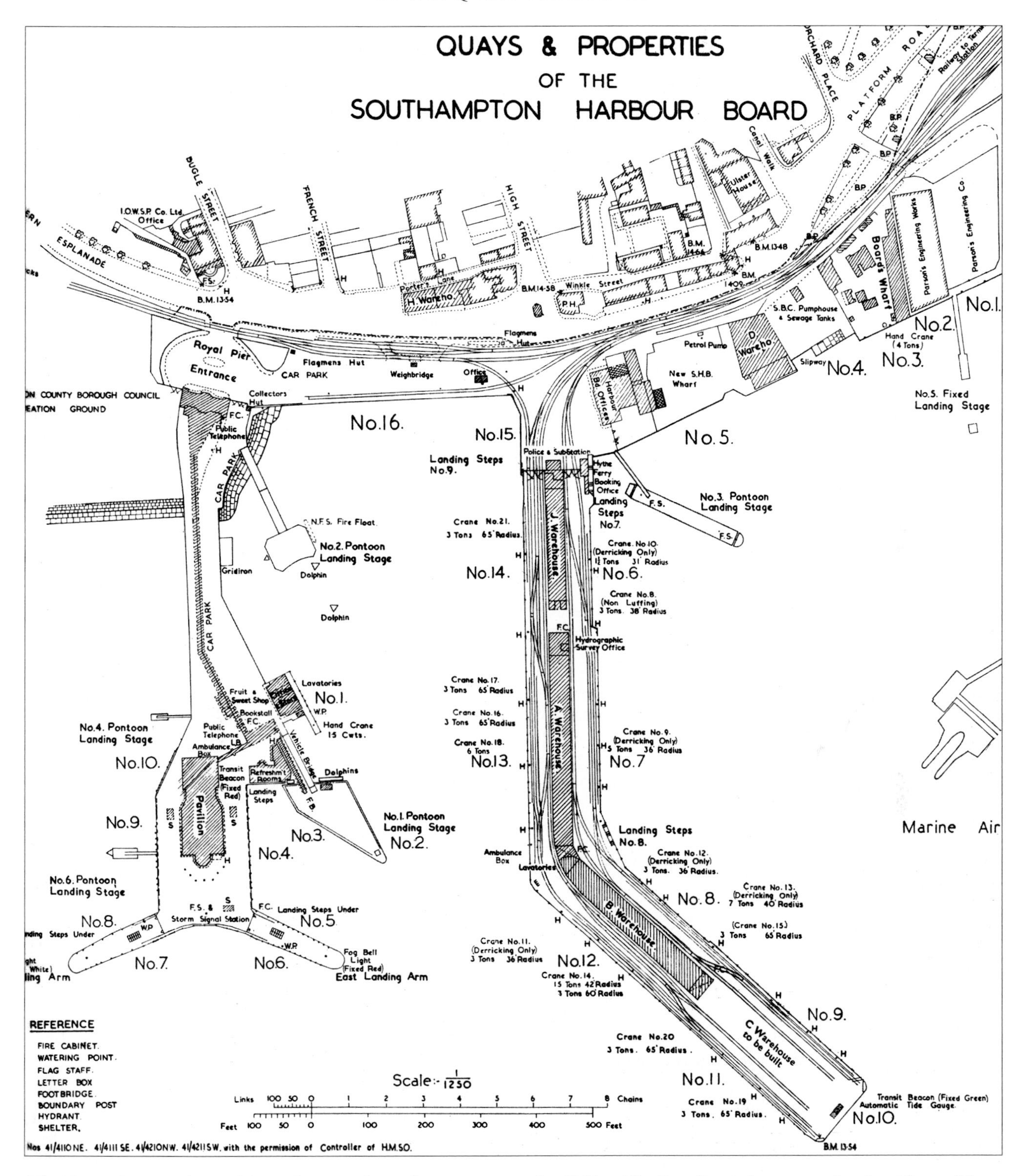

The Town Quay and Royal Pier showing the railway system in the 1950s. The Pier line is long gone, but is still possible to visualize its course to the old station that was adjacent to berth No 1.

Town Quay 0-4-0ST Hawthorn Leslie No 2174 *Clausentum*

Name:	*Clausentum*
Manufacturer:	R. & W. Hawthorn Leslie & Co Ltd, Newcastle-on-Tyne
Built:	1890
Running numbers:	457, 0457, 734 (all LSWR), E374 (SR)
At the Town Quay:	1906–1924

Clausentum was originally built for the Southampton Dock Company in 1890, and came to the Town Quay via the Royal Pier service in 1906. From then, it alternated duties with several other locomotives until taking up its role as shed pilot at Guildford in 1924.

For full details of this loco see Chapter 1.

Town Quay LSWR Class C14 2-2-0T No 744

Manufacturer:	LSWR, Nine Elms Works
Built:	1907
Running numbers:	744, 0744 (both LSWR), 3744 (SR), 30589 (BR)
At the Town Quay:	1911–1917, 1920–1923 and 1948–1957

Built in January 1907 for motor tank working with a trailing passenger coach, class C14 No 744 initially ran on the Portland branch. By 1911 it was a regular at the Town Quay, with weekend duties on the Royal Pier service to Southampton West (now Central) station via the terminus. It was then sent on loan to the Royal Navy depot at Bedenham from January 1917 until February 1920, when it was transferred back to the Town Quay (to partner No 0741).

Like others of the class it was rebuilt as an 0-4-0T in October 1923, and worked in the docks during the 1930s. Under British Railways it was renumbered 30589 in August 1948, and shared Town Quay duties with sister engine 30588 until condemned in June 1957, when it was replaced by another member of the class, No 77s from Redbridge Wharf (see Chapter 10).

Town Quay LSWR Class C14 2-2-0T No 743

Manufacturer:	LSWR, Nine Elms Works
Built:	1906
Running numbers:	743, 0743 (both LSWR)
At the Town Quay:	1913-1915

Class C14 No 743 was built in December 1906, originally for motor tank working with a trailing passenger coach, and ran on the Lymington branch, until transferred to the Bournemouth area in 1911. By July 1912, it was hauling construction materials at Eastleigh Works, where it was rebuilt as an 0-4-0T in June 1913 to join No 745 at the Town Quay. Then, in January 1915, this loco became shed pilot at Guildford.

In March 1917, it was loaned to the Admiralty at Portsmouth Dockyard, who eventually purchased it in November that year. Its last British sighting was in February 1923 at Plantation Quay, Glasgow awaiting shipment to Bombay.

Clausentum in an off-duty moment at Eastleigh. (Bert Moody Collection)

Class C14 No 30589 on an enthusiasts special at Bishops Waltham on 14th June 1952. (Southern Images)

No 30589 in action at the Town Quay on 30th June 1953. (B.K.B. Green)

Town Quay LBSCR Class A1 0-6-0T No 646

Name:	(*Newington*)
Manufacturer:	LBSCR, Brighton Works
Built:	1877
Running numbers:	646 (LBSCR), 734 (LSWR), 2 (FYNR), W2 (SR), 32646 (BR)
Cylinders:	14in x 20in
Driving wheels:	4ft 0in
Wheelbase:	12ft 0in
Working pressure:	150psi
Tank capacity:	500gal
Weight:	26ton 3cwt
At the Town Quay:	1912–1913

Class A1 No 646 named *Newington* was dispatched from Brighton Works in January 1877 for work in the London area, based at New Cross. It became one of two "Terriers" purchased by the LSWR in 1903, due to a shortage of suitable locos to work the Axminster to Lyme Regis branch line. As LSWR No 734, it lost its name and remained in the West Country until transferred to the Portsmouth area in the middle of 1909.

By the end of 1911, it was at Eastleigh for reboilering, and in September the following year, it left the works and took up duties shunting at the Town Quay and Town (Terminus) Station yard. These it performed until the summer of 1913, when it was transferred to the Isle of Wight on the 25th June to work on hire to the Freshwater Yarmouth & Newport Railway as their No 2 until purchased by them in February 1915.

It was then absorbed into the Southern Railway at the grouping of 1923, and was renumbered as W2 by the SR in March 1924. In October 1928 it was renamed, this time as *Freshwater*, but by April 1932 yet another change saw it numbered W8. Nationalisation saw it again nameless, as a return to the mainland in May 1949 brought the final metamorphosis as BR No 32646, applied in August that year.

It returned to Fratton and thence to the Hayling Island branch, until a spell in the Brighton and Newhaven area preceded its withdrawal in November 1963, but that was not the end. It was purchased by the Sadler Rail Car Co for use on the Meon Valley line, where experimental vehicles were being tested, but by May 1966 it had been sold to Brickwoods Brewery, who put it on static display outside one of their public houses on Hayling Island, where it was refurbished once again as LBSCR No 46 *Newington*.

Its role as a glorified pub sign ended in June 1979, when new brewery owners Whitbread spruced it up before handing over to the Wight Locomotive Society. It can now be seen regularly in action on the Isle of Wight Steam Railway.

Former "Brighton Terrier" No 734 poses in its new guise for the LSWR at Nine Elms in 1903. (J.B. Ashford)

Town Quay LSWR Class C14 2-2-0T No 741

Manufacturer:	LSWR, Nine Elms Works
Built:	1906
Running numbers:	741, 0741 (both LSWR), 3741 (SR), 30588 (BR)
At the Town Quay:	1920–1957

C14 No 741 was built in November 1906 for motor tank working with a trailing passenger coach, and worked the on the Southampton Terminus to Winchester service until allocated light shunting duties in 1911. By 1912, the loco was stored at Nine Elms, but in March 1915, it was again working as a motor tank transporting workmen between Bournemouth and Holton Heath where a new Government Cordite Factory was under construction.

In July 1917, it was hired by the Admiralty at Portsmouth Dockyard until November 1919, after which it was sent to the Town Quay (joining No 745) in early 1920. Numbered 0741 in December 1921, and rebuilt as an 0-4-0T in March 1922, it worked regularly at Southampton Docks (with 0744). Renumbered 3741 in 1931, during its Southern Railway days, it entered BR stock at Nationalisation and became No 30588 in December 1950. It then worked as the Town Quay shunter until condemned in December1957, when its place was taken by sister engine 77s from Redbridge Wharf (see Chapter 10).

Class C14 No 741 in SR days as No 3741 at the Town Quay. (Bert Moody Collection)

Town Quay LSWR Class C14 2-2-0T No 745

Manufacturer:	LSWR, Nine Elms Works
Built:	1907
Running numbers:	745, 0745 (both LSWR), 3745 (SR), 77s (BR Departmental)
At the Town Quay:	1913–1927 and 1957-1959

Class C14 No 745 was built in January 1907 originally as a 2-2-0T for motor tank working between Plymouth Friary and St. Budeaux, but by 1911 it had been transferred to the Bournemouth area. By July 1912, it was at Eastleigh Works hauling construction materials (with No 743) before being rebuilt as an 0-4-0T in April 1913. It was then dispatched to regular duties at the Town Quay (again sharing duties with No 743) and was still a regular there during World War I, where it was joined by sister engines 0741 and 0744 early in 1920.

In October 1927 it was renumbered 77s when transferred to the Engineer's Department, and was sent to work at Redbridge Wharf (see Chapter 10), where it saw continuous service until moving back to the Town Quay in 1957 as a replacement for Nos 0741 and 0744 after that pair had been condemned. There it saw out its final years until being scrapped in April 1959 as the last member of its class.

The final C14 performs at Town Quay as 77s returns to the Platform Road sidings in December 1957. (I.J. Bovey)

Class C14 No 745 as Departmental No 77s takes a final turn of duty at the Town Quay in January 1959. (Author's Collection)

CHAPTER 8

Royal Pier Railway 1871-1915

By an Act of Parliament of 1803 the Southampton Harbour Commissioners were empowered to administer the affairs of the port and to improve quay facilities along the lower town. This included the construction of a new pier, opened in 1833 by Princess Victoria, to accommodate steam packets from France and the Channel Islands. Following the completion of the London and Southampton Railway (subsequently the LSWR) in 1840, passengers were conveyed from the Town Station (later Southampton Terminus) to the Victoria Pier by horse-drawn omnibus,

A tramway, also horse-drawn, had been laid to the Town Quay in 1847 (see Chapter 7) and this was leased to the LSWR from 1851. In 1864, improvements were made to the Pier where passengers were now embarking for pleasure trips to the Isle of Wight and South Coast resorts. To accommodate this ever increasing trade the railway company extended the Town Quay tracks westwards to the Pier in 1871, and then sought to augment the service by approaching the town council for permission to operate the line with steam power.

After some misgivings by the Board of Trade, trials were carried out by one of the Dock Company locos, *Sir Bevis*, in 1876. These went well, and an agreement was reached, but with severe limitations to the locomotive's speed, weight, noise, exhaust emissions, and with the proviso that the public should be protected by it being proceeded by a man with a bell and flag on road crossings. To meet these strict criteria, the LSWR ordered a small condensing tank loco from Alexander Shanks & Sons of Arbroath. Appropriately named *Southampton*, it commenced service in September 1876.

Such was its success that a second engine was ordered the following year from the same manufacturer. *Cowes* arrived for duty in November 1877, and formed a winning partnership with *Southampton*, until December 1879 when a third locomotive was required. By coincidence, a similar locomotive by the same builder, named *Ritzebuttel*, was for sale at Southampton Docks, having just returned with three others from a construction contract at Cuxhaven Harbour. Thus, the three diminutive tank locomotives worked the Royal Pier passenger services together with occasional shunting duties at the Town Quay.

At this time, the station at the seaward end of the Pier consisted of just a simple open platform until, in 1892, the entire wooden structure was substantially rebuilt in iron and enlarged to become the Royal Pier – the biggest such leisure facility on the south coast of England. To enhance

The Victoria Pier in 1880 shows the original open wooden railway platform. (Hume Family Collection / University of Queensland)

its new stature, a more commodious station was built having two platforms, each complete with canopies to shelter passengers from the elements.

The LSWR, having purchased the docks in 1892, maintained the Dock Company and Royal Pier locomotives in their docks workshops until 1898, when the fleet became part of the railway company's general stock.

As the Southampton Dock Company locomotives were being replaced by B4 tanks, several of their number became surplus and other duties were sought for them. *Bretwalda* was transferred to the Pier in April 1900 after *Ritzebuttel* had been given the less taxing job of shunting at Eastleigh Carriage Works, and a year later, in March 1901, *Clausentum* had taken over from *Cowes*. This pair maintained the run to the Town Station with occasional Town Quay shunting, while *Southampton* was reduced to a standby engine. By October 1902, *Bretwalda* had relocated to Bournemouth, but the other two remained until late 1906, when class C14 motor tanks took over the route. From then on *Clausentum* became permanently based at the Town Quay where it remained until Southern Railway days.

Rail motors were single passenger coaches, each powered by a small integral steam locomotive, and they were the railways' answer to the threat of the electric tram at the beginning of the twentieth century. However, they were largely unsuccessful, and were soon replaced by the more flexible motor trains that had interchangeable locomotives and coaches. On 9th December 1909, the largely redundant rail motors were introduced to the Royal Pier service, initially by class H12 No 1 and class H13 No 11.

The main dimensions of the H12 class were:

Cylinders:	9in x 14in
Driving wheels:	3ft 0in
Wheelbase:	8ft 0in
Working pressure:	150psi
Tank capacity:	530gal
Weight:	31ton 10¾cwt (combined engine and coach)

The new Royal Pier station with a train headed by locomotive "Southampton" sometime after 1892. (Veal Collection / Southampton City Archive)

Sadly, passenger numbers were in decline and No 1 was taken off in December 1912, while the service itself was suspended from the autumn of 1913. The following spring saw a revised schedule, with H13 units being employed there. Most often, Nos 7 or 10 would be in evidence, but others would occasionally turn up. The timetable was now sporadic, and the structure of the Pier railway, and the station itself, had badly deteriorated. The H13 class dimensions differed as follows:

Cylinders:	10in x 14in
Driving wheels:	3ft 0in
Wheelbase:	8ft 0in
Working pressure:	175psi
Tank capacity:	485gal
Weight:	32ton 6 cwt (combined engine and coach)

This situation continued until the outbreak of World War I, when passenger services officially ceased, and No 10 was transferred to Wadebridge. However, it would seem that No 7 remained at the Pier until the following year, after which it was taken out of service and finally broken up in November 1916.

During the war, the line was used for troop movements, but afterwards it seems that a ship had collided with the Pier, causing considerable damage to the railway, which was already in a poor state of repair. Consequently, it was considered too costly to reinstate the track, and the service was never resumed.

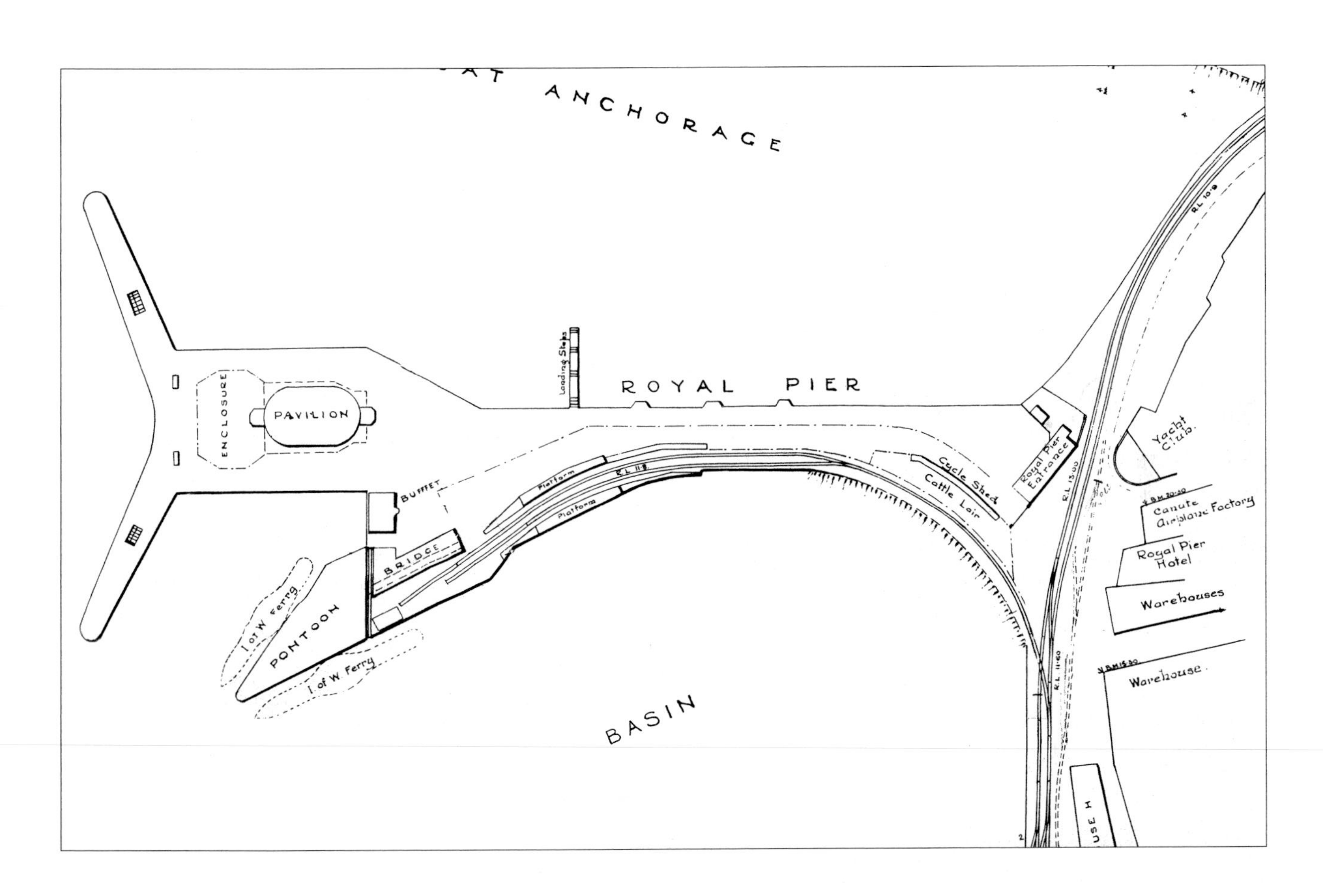

A drawing of the Royal Pier at the end of World War I showing the disused railway and station.

Royal Pier LSWR 0-4-0ST No 109 *Southampton*

Name:	*Southampton*
Manufacturer:	Alexander Shanks & Son, Arbroath
Built:	1876
Running numbers:	109, 0109 (both LSWR)
Cylinders:	10¼in x 20in
Driving wheels:	3ft 0in
Wheelbase:	5ft 6in
Working pressure:	120psi
Tank capacity:	400gal
Weight:	18ton 7½cwt
At the Royal Pier:	1876-1906

Southampton was the first of a trio of Shanks' engines specially commissioned to work the Royal Pier Railway for the LSWR, and it arrived new from the makers in September 1876. This engine had been given the number 109 in January 1898, but following the arrivals of *Bretwalda* (in 1900) and *Clausentum* (in 1901), *Southampton* was reduced to the role of standby engine, occasionally making trips to Poole for the service at Hamworthy. Having been renumbered 0109 in March 1904, it was reunited with 0110 *Ritzebuttel* in February 1905, when working on the construction of the Amesbury Extension Light Railway, but afterwards it saw little employment apart from occasional service as a relief loco back at the Town Quay and Royal Pier until the C14s took over in 1906.

In August 1910, *Southampton* was back at Poole, but by the autumn of 1912 it had been taken out of service. December 1913 saw it condemned at Eastleigh with its two sisters, but wartime saw a reprieve from the scrap heap, and it was eventually sold in December 1915 to Kynock Ltd at Longparish, Hants, where it was finally broken up in 1919.

Royal Pier LSWR 0-4-0ST No 108 *Cowes*

Name:	*Cowes*
Manufacturer:	Alexander Shanks & Son, Arbroath
Built:	1877
Running numbers:	108, 0108 (both LSWR)
Cylinders:	10¼in x 20in
Driving wheels:	3ft 0in
Wheelbase:	5ft 6in
Working pressure:	120psi
Tank capacity:	400gal
Weight:	18ton 7½cwt
At the Royal Pier:	1877-1901

Cowes arrived new to the Royal Pier Railway in November 1877, being the second of the Shanks-built trio to work there. It became numbered 108 by the LSWR in August 1898, and shared the odd shift at the Town Quay until the Shanks' locos were replaced by former Dock Company veterans, first *Bretwalda* in 1900, and then *Clausentum*, which arrived at the Pier in March 1901.

Cowes was renumbered 0108 in March 1904, but was little used until the summers of 1906-7, when it was hired out to the War Department, and used for training Royal Engineers at Christchurch. By December 1913, it was stored at Eastleigh (with sisters *Southampton* and *Ritzebuttel*) where it remained in a condemned state until World War I postponed its scrapping. In April 1915, it was sold to Plenmellor Colliery, Northumberland, and was last seen derelict there in August 1930.

Royal Pier Loco "Southampton" as LSWR No 109 at the Town Station yard in 1902. (C.H. Eden)

Royal Pier locomotive "Cowes" at Nine Elms in March 1906. (Author's Collection)

Royal Pier locomotive "Ritzebuttel" pictured at Eastleigh. (Author's Collection)

Royal Pier LSWR 0-4-0ST No 110 *Ritzebuttel*

Name:	*Ritzebuttel*
Manufacturer:	Alexander Shanks & Son, Arbroath
Built:	1873
Works number:	468
Running numbers:	110, 0110 (both LSWR)
Cylinders:	10in x 20in
Driving wheels:	3ft 0in
Wheelbase:	5ft 6in
Working pressure:	120psi
Tank capacity:	370gal
Weight:	17ton 12¾cwt
At the Royal Pier:	1879-1900

Ritzebuttel was the third Shanks loco acquired by the LSWR for the Royal Pier service, but unlike the other two, it arrived there second-hand. Having been built in 1873, it previously worked in Germany during the construction of Cuxhaven Harbour. On its return home, it was auctioned, along with three other Shanks' locomotives, at Southampton Docks, where it was purchased for £450 in December 1879.

In August 1898, it had been numbered 110, but in April 1900, it had been displaced on the Pier by former Dock Company loco *Bretwalda*, and was sent to shunt the yards at Eastleigh Carriage Works. Another change of number (to 0110) came in March 1904, but *Ritzebuttel* found little employment until January 1905, when it was used in the construction of the Amesbury Extension Light Railway. There, it was reunited with former Pier running mate 0109 *Southampton* in the following month.

After this, it saw little further activity apart from a spell of duty at Exmouth Docks in May 1911, and it was finally taken out of service in December 1913 and condemned at Eastleigh with sister engines *Southampton* and *Cowes*. The impending war having postponed its demise, it was sold in December 1915 to the Witton works of Kynock Ltd, Birmingham. It continued working there until advertised for sale in July 1921 and was scrapped soon afterwards.

See page 113 for an illustration of this locomotive.

Royal Pier 0-4-0ST Hawthorn Leslie No 2174 *Clausentum*

Name:	*Clausentum*
Manufacturer:	R. & W. Hawthorn Leslie & Co Ltd, Newcastle-on-Tyne
Built:	1890
Running numbers:	457, 0457, 734 (all LSWR), E374 (SR)
At the Royal Pier:	1901-1906

Clausentum was originally built for the Southampton Dock Company in 1890, and came to the Royal Pier service in 1901 after being made redundant in the docks with the arrival of the B4 tanks. At the Pier, it joined Shanks' locomotive *Southampton* and former SDC running mate, *Bretwalda*. The latter was transferred within a year, and the remaining pair shared the duties until 1906, when they were replaced by C14 motor tanks, and *Clausentum* was sent to the Town Quay.

For full details of this loco see Chapter 1.

Royal Pier 0-4-0ST Vulcan No 837 *Bretwalda*

Name:	*Bretwalda*
Manufacturer:	Vulcan Foundry Ltd, Newton-le-Willows, Lancashire.
Built:	1878
Running numbers:	408, 0408, (both LSWR), E0408 (SR)
At the Royal Pier:	1900-1901

Former Southampton Dock Co locomotive, *Bretwalda*, came to the Royal Pier service in April 1900 after the arrival of the B4 tanks at its previous home. Here, it replaced Shanks' loco *Ritzebuttel*, which had been transferred to Eastleigh Carriage Works. However, by the following October it had again been relocated, this time to Bournemouth.

For full details of this loco see Chapter 1.

Royal Pier LSWR Class H12 Rail Motor Car No 1

Manufacturer: LSWR, Nine Elms
Built: 1904
Running numbers: 1
At the Royal Pier: 1909-1912

Rail motor car No 1 was built in May 1904, and began life on the Basingstoke and Alton Light Railway before first moving to Bournemouth, and then to Bishops Waltham in October that same year. In May 1906, it was on trial with the military between Aldershot and Alton until going on loan to the Somerset and Dorset Joint Railway in August 1906, but it returned to general service after only a brief summer season there, and resumed the Botley to Bishops Waltham service.

In December 1909 it was used on the Royal Pier rail motor service with H13 class No 11, where it appeared regularly until December 1912, when it was transferred to Strawberry Hill. There, it worked between Gunnersbury and Twickenham until taken out of service in October 1914 and laid up at Eastleigh before being scrapped in November 1916.

Royal Pier LSWR Class H13 Rail Motor Car No 7

Manufacturer: LSWR, Nine Elms
Built: 1906
Running numbers: 7
At the Royal Pier: 1914-1915

The H13 class rail motors improved on several features of the earlier H12s, with better ventilation, less engine noise and more passenger accommodation. Built in January 1906, No 7 was initially sent for trials on the Botley to Bishops Waltham line before being transferred to the Plymouth Friary to Turnchapel service soon afterwards.

By early 1907, it had moved to Guildford until being replaced there by motor tanks in 1910, and by July 1914, it had joined several others of the class sharing the duties at the Royal Pier. Although the Pier service was officially suspended at the outbreak of World War I, it appears that No 7 might have remained there until the middle of 1915, possibly engaged in troop movements. It was finally taken out of service and scrapped in November of the following year.

A typical class H13 rail motor pictured at Eastleigh around 1910. Thirteen were built during 1905-6, but all had been withdrawn by 1916. (Author's Collection)

Royal Pier LSWR Class H13 Rail Motor Car No 10

Manufacturer:	LSWR, Nine Elms
Built:	1906
Running numbers:	10
At the Royal Pier:	1914

Having been built in March 1906, and after completing its trials on the Botley to Bishops Waltham line, H13 class No 10 was transferred to Guildford for work on the Bordon Branch on 1st June that year. By August 1909, it had moved to Lee-on-the-Solent but was soon replaced there by No 9, and stored out of use at Eastleigh until the summer of 1914, when it joined others of the class on the Royal Pier service.

When the Pier service closed, it was sent Wadebridge, remaining there until June 1916 went it moved to Bodmin, its final duty before withdrawal in March 1918 and being scrapped in July 1919.

Class H13 rail motor No 10 pictured in its early days. (TLP Collection)

Royal Pier LSWR Class H13 Rail Motor Car No 11

Manufacturer:	LSWR, Nine Elms
Built:	1906
Running numbers:	11
At the Royal Pier:	1909-1914

Class H13 No 11 entered service in March 1906, and after initial trials on the Botley to Bishops Waltham line, was employed at Andover Junction for the Whitchurch to Fullerton service from 1st June that year.

By 9th December 1909, it had been transferred to the Royal Pier to initiate a rail motor service together with class H12 No 1, after which it made occasional visits in turn with others of the class, until the summer of 1914 saw it take on its final duties at Bishops Waltham, Wadebridge, and Gunnersbury, before being condemned and taken out of service in November 1916. As with many of the rail motors, the carriage section was afterwards converted to a trailer coach for motor train working.

CHAPTER 9

Train Ferries 1917-1922 and 1943-1946

During World War I, the Government sought ways of transferring supplies more quickly to the British troops in Europe, and considered that train ferries would speed the process greatly if rail-mounted provisions, arms and munitions could be shunted directly on and off vessels at either side of the channel.

Several UK sites were examined, and Southampton was one of two locations chosen after consideration by the War Cabinet in 1917 (the other being at Richborough in Kent). The Southampton terminal was built to the west of the existing Royal Pier, and was connected by a branch line running along the Western Shore from the south side of the LSWR main line station at Southampton West.

The line was constructed by the military, and involved considerable reclamation of the shoreline to provide land for sidings and marshalling yards on the approach to the ferry pier. The Royal Engineers track ran parallel to Western Esplanade, which was closed to the general public, and at the southern end, a stone embankment was built out to the jetty where a wooden bridge carried the tracks out to the ships that berthed against a linkspan, to enable loading at all states of the tide.

Construction began in August 1917, and was finally completed by the following February when the "main line" double track ran through the marshalling yards to the terminal, about a mile in length overall. Seven sidings were provided at the station end adjacent to the power station, while to the south of the Pirelli works, twelve more could accommodate up to 500 wagons. A further eight berthing sidings, capable of holding another 200 wagons completed the complex, which straddled the Pirelli factory. It included an oil storage facility where four large tanks held fuel brought in by tanker trains. From here there was a pipe connection along the jetty to the ships.

A two-road locomotive shed was constructed just south of the Pirelli works, at the northern end of the main yard, and the task of the two inhabitants was to make up the trains ready for each vessel's call, along with general loading and unloading duties. One engine was a Kerr Stuart "Victory" class 0-6-0T (works No 3067) built in May 1917. This was No 11 of the Inland Waterways and Docks Department, operated by the military, and would have been used primarily during the construction works. The line itself was extended past the Royal Pier by double tracks to the Town Quay so that military barges could be loaded there. The other locomotive was an unidentified Peckett 0-4-0ST that features in several photos of the facility in operation.

On board the ferries, four rail tracks could each accommodate about a dozen wagons. These were laid on the decks with timber packing enabling the surface to be made flush with the tops of the rails, so that land vehicles could also be driven on and off. Initially, there were three ferries operating on the route from Southampton to Dieppe, these alternating with the service from Richborough.

The whole complex was operated by the military, who were housed in accommodation and offices on-site, with traffic movements being carried out by train ferry personnel under their supervision. LSWR locomotives would bring in and take out the assembled trains in each direction from the main line at Southampton West.

With wartime activities escalating, and each vessel

The ferry pier and terminal seen from Western Esplanade. (Southampton City Archive)

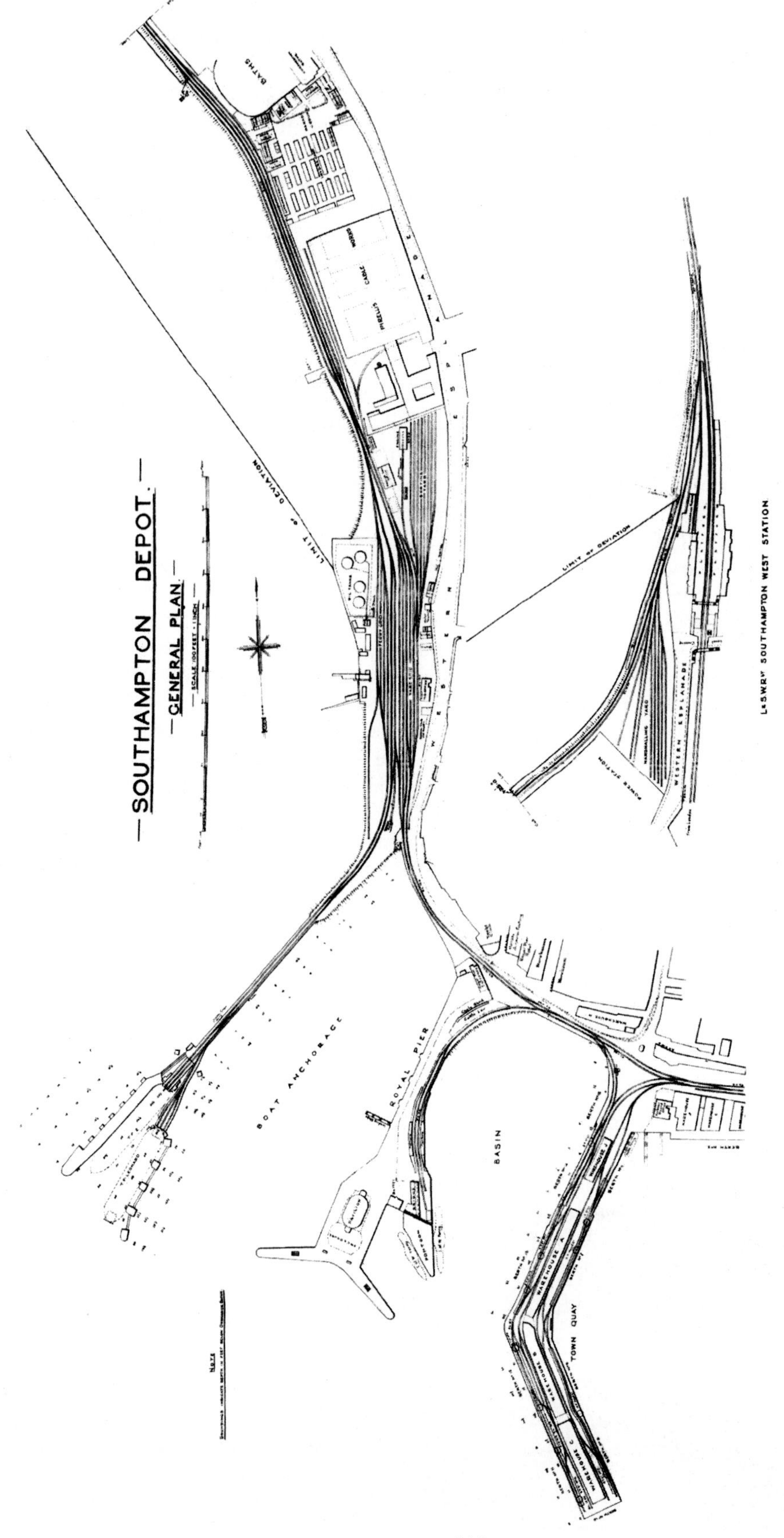

General plan of the Southampton terminal, showing the sidings and marshalling yards on the approach to the ferry pier. (Author's Collection)

already running up to a dozen trips each month, a fourth vessel was urgently required by the spring of 1918, and a secondary route was opened up to Cherbourg.

The scale of the operation is reflected in the equipment carried back and forth. The total shipped out from Southampton was 8 locomotives, 42 coaches and 6,763 wagons, while the return journeys saw 272 engines and 1250 wagons being carried.

After hostilities ceased, the ferries continued to run from Southampton to Dieppe and Cherbourg until March 1919, after which the vessels were laid up and some thought was given to future use of the facility. There was an idea that the LSWR might use it for civilian passengers, but nothing came of it and other organisations were sounded out.

If the line and jetty was not used for a ferry, perhaps it could be utilised in other ways? One of the main problems was a dispute over who owned what, with land and equipment having either been built by, or commandeered by the military, and other areas were still owned by private or civic bodies. For instance, Pirelli had a jetty that couldn't be used because it had been cut off from the works by the ferry sidings, but they had gained sidings of their own that could no longer be used if the line was taken up. Even the public roadway remained closed until the issues could be resolved.

The prevarications continued for many months, and interest began to wane. By the summer of 1920, the Admiralty was using the pier to lay up ships, but was reluctant to take over any of the other facilities, and this conflict with the military also deterred any mildly interested parties.

Eventually in 1921, the War Department decided to remove it all, but the costs were prohibitive, and there were still the disputes over land and property that dragged on for another two years. The track was taken up, possibly by the following year, but it wasn't until September 1923 that the linkspan was sold and dismantled. It was then placed on barges for relocation to Harwich, where a new train ferry was to operate to Zeebrugge in Belgium, but the miserable chain of events continued when the barges sank en route.

Removal of the jetty piles would call for an expert (and expensive) process. It was therefore still *in situ* by 1927, when events were under way to build the New Docks extension for the Southern Railway. This huge project saw the reclamation of over 400 acres of the adjacent West Bay mudlands, and the remnants of the ferry terminal finally disappeared beneath it all, mainly under the present Mayflower Park.

Due to the vast scale and cost of the project, the outstanding "loose ends" were quickly settled. The rail spur from Southampton West station was revived until 1929 for contractor's trains running reclamation materials, after which these were brought in via a rail connection from the Old (Eastern) Docks.

However, that was not the final chapter for Southampton train ferries as World War II saw their reintroduction at two locations – one at the Town Quay, adjacent to, and just east of the Royal Pier, the other at 110 berth alongside the King George V Graving Dock (No 7 Drydock). These were once again operated by the military, who used War Department locomotives.

After the war, proposals were made to establish a permanent train ferry service from Southampton to Le Havre, but due to war damage across the channel, the plans were first delayed and then abandoned.

The disused train ferry jetty was later used during the construction of the new docks, when ships carrying cement bags discharged onto wagons for processing at the concrete mixing station erected nearby. This photograph was taken on 26th February 1930. (Associated British Ports)

Above: This aerial view appeared in a Southern Railway book called "A Souvenir of Southampton Docks" that was published in 1930, during the construction of the New (Western) Docks. It shows, from left to right, the Train Ferry Terminal , the Royal Pier and the Town Quay. (Author's Collection)

Left: The ferry deck showing on-board tracks that were levelled with timber packing to allow road vehicles easy access. (Royal Engineers Library, Chatham)

An ambulance train being loaded at the 110 berth ferry terminal in World War II. (Author's Collection)

War Department loco No 179 (ex-GWR No 2466) loading ferries adjacent to the Royal Pier in 1944. (The wartime censor had obliterated parts of this photo as a matter of security.) (ABP / Southampton City Archive)

IW&D "Victory" Class 0-6-0T Kerr Stuart No 3067

Manufacturer:	Kerr Stuart & Co Ltd, Stoke on Trent, Staffs
Works number:	3067
Built:	1917
Running numbers:	11 (IW&D), 610 (ROD), 4 (EKR), 30948 (BR)
Cylinders:	17in x 24in
Driving wheels:	4ft 0in
Wheelbase:	12ft 0in
Tank capacity:	970gal
Weight:	49ton 0cwt
At the Train Ferry:	1917-1919

No 3067 was supplied new by Kerr Stuart to the Royal Engineers for the construction of the Inland Waterways & Docks Train Ferry at Southampton, where it ran as No 11. Following completion of the works, it remained on-site until moving to a similar installation at Richborough, Kent by October 1919, where under the Railway Operating Department, it took the number 610. After service there, it was sold to the East Kent Railway in 1920 where it became their No 4, working through the Southern Railway years and into Nationalisation, when it was allocated British Railways number 30948. However, this was never applied, and the locomotive was scrapped at Ashford in February 1949.

IW&D No 11 standing near the Train Ferry loco shed in June 1917. (Royal Engineers Library, Chatham)

IW&D Peckett 0-4-0ST

Manufacturer:	Peckett & Sons, Atlas Works, Bristol
At the Train Ferry:	1917-1919

Little is known about the Peckett loco that worked on loading and unloading the Southampton train ferries. As in many wartime situations, it was probably working for an industrial concern in the region before being commandeered by the military for service in the national interest.

A glimpse of the unidentified Peckett locomotive on the train ferry jetty circa 1918. (Author's Collection)

CHAPTER 10

Redbridge Wharf 1880-1989

By 1847, the Southampton & Dorchester Railway had been laid through Totton and Redbridge, and four years later it had become amalgamated with the LSWR. The old wharf at Redbridge had been a rural backwater where, apart from a little shipbuilding, goods where transhipped to the quayside from barges on the old Andover Canal. In 1851, the S&D had built a tramway from its main line at Totton to Eling Wharf, and the LSWR had subsequently used this for importing timber for railway sleepers and various other components for tracklaying, but in 1880 they purchased the wharf and premises at Redbridge, and switched their operations to the new site.

Development of the wharf and the construction of new sidings soon followed, along with the installation of large creosote tanks for treating the timber sleepers. There were a number of other commercial premises that had developed at the wharf, one being the already established Dixon & Cardus oil-seed mill, and another, the Schultz Gunpowder Works built in 1897 – at a safe distance from the other activities! There was also a disused chemical works, which closed in 1892. All were served by sidings, with main line engines working the goods traffic to them.

The railway company eventually took over and adapted these buildings as their own operations increased. In 1899 Dixon and Cardus transferred operations to their other premises at Northam Quay (see Chapter 15), and the LSWR converted its works into a sawmill. The gunpowder factory was taken over by the Royal Navy during World War I, and finally closed in 1922, the buildings eventually being purchased by the railway (by then SR) in 1926.

From the days of the Southern Railway, Redbridge Depot was at first solely concerned with the manufacture and distribution of sleepers, but it later expanded its operations to include the production and assembly of prefabricated rail sections with materials arriving by rail and sea. It built its own foundry, and continuously adapted its processes in line with modern technology, one of the biggest changes coming in the 1960s when the traditional wooden sleepers gave way to the reinforced concrete variety.

Rail wagons were originally moved about by the steam cranes that unloaded the ships and barges, but as the works expanded, the need came for some more versatile form of motive power. Occasional shunting was carried

The old Dixon & Cardus works converted to a sawmill and pictured in 1924. (British Railways)

out by locomotives loaned from the docks, but in 1927, it was decided that the yard would have its own engine. A trio of diminutive C14 class 0-4-0Ts were employed in shunting duties at the Town Quay, and one of these, No 745, was transferred to service stock and sent to Redbridge as No 77s in October of that year. An old pump house, adjacent to the main line, was converted into a loco shed, and became "home" to a succession of shunters over the years.

77s remained there for some thirty years until recalled to the Town Quay in 1957. At that time, Eastleigh had various spare tank locos biding their time surplus to normal requirements, and these included the remnants of the O2 class 0-4-4Ts that had mostly gone to the scrapheap during the 1950s. Of those that remained, a few were used to cover the vacant duties at Redbridge. In fact, one or two had already been sent there as replacements when 77s was off for repair. Their main dimensions were:

Cylinders:	17½in x 24in
Driving wheels:	4ft 10in
Trailing wheels:	3ft 0in
Working pressure:	160psi
Tank capacity:	800gal
Weight:	46ton 18cwt

No 30199 became a regular at Redbridge until replaced in October 1962, and this proved to be its final assignment, as it was withdrawn and broken up in December that year. Others of the same class recorded there between 1957 and 1962 included Nos 30212 and 30229. Another O2, No 30225, was engaged as occasional shed pilot at Eastleigh while 30199 was at Redbridge, so there is every possibility that it was also sent there as relief engine during that period.

The O2s, however, did not prove entirely successful and trials were made to find a more permanent replacement. The USA 0-6-0Ts at Southampton Docks were being replaced by diesels, and one of their number, 30061, was drafted to the wharf in October 1962 as Departmental loco No DS233. The USA was almost twice the size of the C14, but still managed to squeeze inside the stone-built shed until March 1967, when dieselisation came to Redbridge.

Steam cranes were a common mode of locomotion in 1926. (British Railways)

Production at the works moved to continuous-welded rails, and the creosoting plant with its tanks and storage areas was closed and demolished by the late 1970s. By now, the depot's machine shops were turning out sections of switches, crossovers, and preassembled points sections, in fact, every component needed for track laying and maintenance.

For so many years, Redbridge works had been a commercial success, but a change in national railway policy in the 1980s meant that track would be manufactured and bought in from outside contractors, thus the depot's end was in sight, and by the time of its closure, in March 1989, it had become the last railway-owned permanent way manufacturing depot in England.

A century of creosote, gunpowder, and a host of chemicals had left their marks on the environment, and the soil at the depot went through a lengthy process of decontamination after Associated British Ports purchased the land in March 1994. Most of the area is now used as storage for the import and export of motor vehicles, but one small section at the Western end was converted to a riverside park and given over to the City Council in September 2002. A small derrick crane was retained on the site, and now stands at the water's edge as the only visible reminder of the wharf's history.

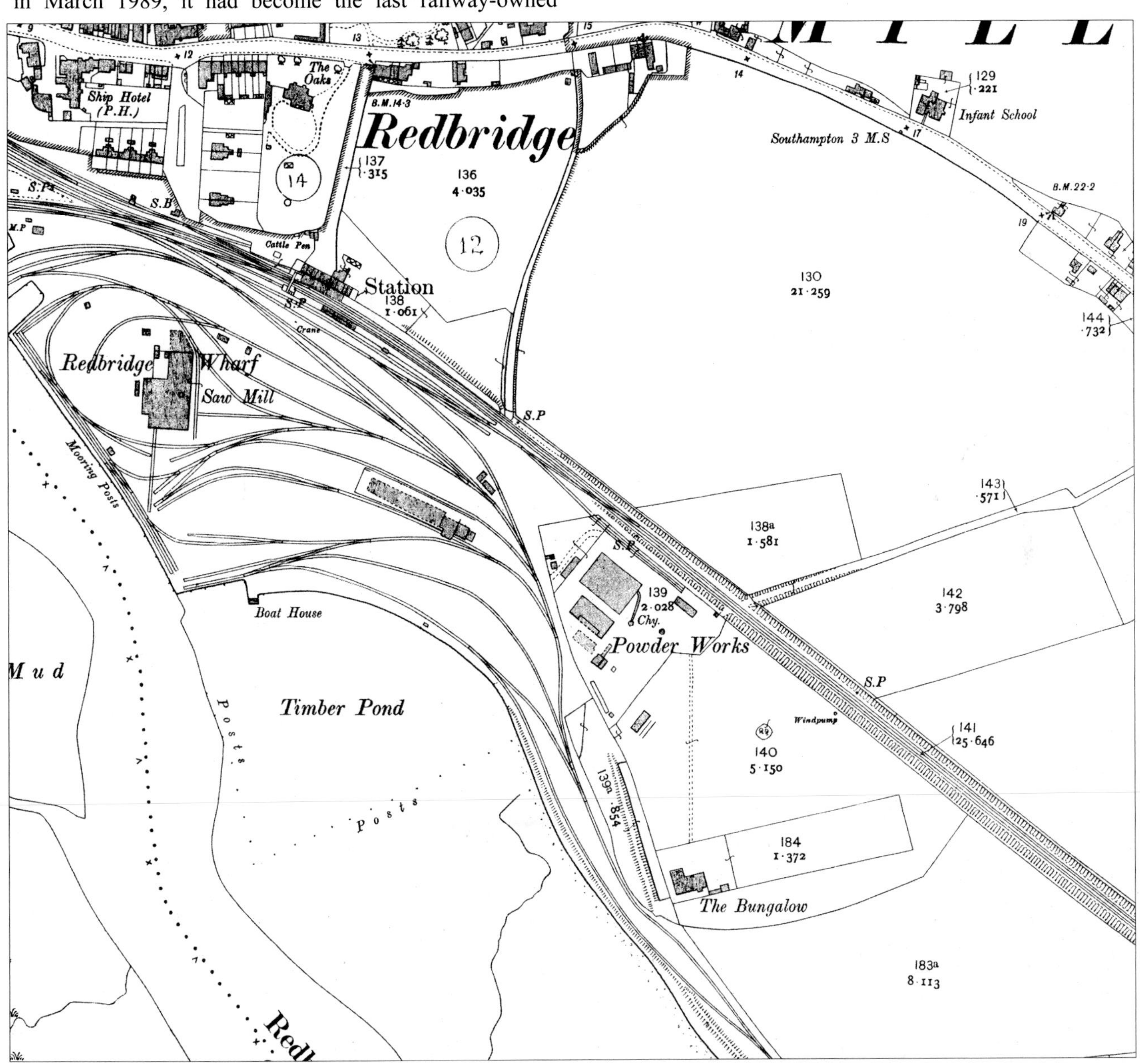

Early railway days at Redbridge Wharf – the general layout in 1910. (Reproduced from 1910 Ordnance Survey map with the kind permission of the Ordnance Survey.)

Redbridge Wharf LSWR Class C14 0-4-0T No 77s

Manufacturer:	LSWR, Nine Elms Works
Built:	1907
Running numbers:	745, 0745 (both LSWR), 3745 (SR), 77s (Departmental)
At Redbridge Wharf:	1927-1957

Originally built in January 1907 as a 2-2-0T for motor tank working with a trailing passenger coach, and based in the Plymouth area. By 1911, it had been transferred to Bournemouth, and in July 1912 it was at Eastleigh Works, before being rebuilt as an 0-4-0T in April 1913. From then, it was on regular duty at the Town Quay with others of the same class, remaining there for many years until renumbered 77s in October 1927, when it was transferred to the Engineer's Department and sent to Redbridge Wharf. There it saw service until 1957, when it was recalled to the Town Quay, seeing out its final years there until being scrapped in April 1959. For full details of this loco see Chapter 7.

Redbridge Wharf LWSR Class O2 0-4-4T No 30199

Manufacturer:	LSWR, Nine Elms Works
Built:	1891
Running numbers:	199 (LSWR), 30199 (BR)
At Redbridge Wharf:	1957–1962 (periodical)

Built in June 1891 as one of a once numerous LSWR class of motor trains for suburban passenger services in the London area, but later dispersed over the SR system. During World War II, No 30199 was working as a temporary replacement on the Lyme Regis branch, and by April 1950, it had become stationed at Exmouth Junction, working the local trains to Exmouth. Whilst there, occasional visits were paid to Meldon Quarry as relief engine for the usual departmental locomotive.

As the class was gradually culled in the later 1950s, No 30199 found itself transferred to Eastleigh, and from there became one of a number of the class acting as Redbridge Depot shunter after the regular loco, departmental No 77s, was relocated to the Town Quay in 1957. The O2's appearances at Redbridge ceased when USA No 30061 was transferred to the Engineer's Department and sent there permanently as No DS233 in October 1962. Within two months, No 30199 had been withdrawn from service and scrapped.

Redbridge Wharf LSWR Class O2 0-4-4T No 30229

Manufacturer:	LSWR, Nine Elms Works
Built:	1894
Running numbers:	229 (LSWR, 30229 (BR)
At Redbridge Wharf:	1957–1961 (periodical)

Built in December 1894 by the LSWR, this loco remained in the Clapham area unlike others of the class that were dispersed over the SR system, and it was still in that vicinity by 1932. Wartime service saw it transferred to the Portland Branch, and by 1950 it was at Dorchester.

Like the other remnants of the class, its closing years were spent at Eastleigh, where it was occasionally steamed for duty at the docks and at Redbridge, after the regular locomotive, departmental No 77s, had been sent to the Town Quay in 1957. The end came in March 1961, when it was withdrawn from service and scrapped.

C14 class departmental locomotive No 77s in Southern Railway days at Redbridge Works. (W.M.J. Jackson)

O2 No 30199 at Eastleigh in May 1952. (R.K. Blencowe Collection)

O2 No 30229 passes the Town Quay bound for the Eastern Docks. (TLP Collection)

Redbridge Wharf LSWR Class O2 0-4-4T No 30212

Manufacturer:	LSWR, Nine Elms Works
Built:	1892
Running numbers:	212 (LSWR), 30212 (BR)
At Redbridge Wharf:	1957–1959 (periodical)

Built in May 1892 working motor trains on suburban passenger services in the London area. During World War II, No 212 was in regular service around the Clapham Junction area, but by 1950 it was stationed at Bournemouth. Its final years were spent mostly idle at Eastleigh, where it was occasionally steamed for duty at Redbridge, rotating with the few surviving remnants of the class from 1957, after the regular locomotive, Departmental No 77s had been relocated to the Town Quay. This was its final duty until being laid aside in December 1959 and scrapped.

Redbridge Wharf LSWR Class O2 0-4-4T No 30225

Manufacturer:	LSWR, Nine Elms Works
Built:	1892
Running numbers:	225 (LSWR), 30225 (BR)
At Redbridge Wharf:	1957–1962 (periodical)

Built in November 1892 by the LSWR, by Southern Railway days, No 225 had been posted to Plymouth where it worked the Callington and Turnchapel services, and by the early 1930s it had been transferred to Yeovil. However, between 1941 and 1943, it was on loan to the War Department, during which time it was reported as being in an extremely poor state in the GWR yard at Oxford. By November the following year, it had been returned to the SR via the Bicester WD depot.

By 1950, No 30225 was stationed at Eastleigh, where it was still regularly working passenger services in 1960, and by 1962 it was one of only two class members still working on the mainland (the other being 30199). After the regular Redbridge departmental locomotive, No 77s, had been transferred to Town Quay duties 1957, O2s based at Eastleigh were drafted there periodically until a permanent replacement (USA DS233) was found in October 1962. No 30225, as one of a dwindling band that performed this duty before being withdrawn and scrapped in December 1962.

Redbridge Wharf SR USA Class 0-6-0T No DS233

Manufacturer:	H.K. Porter, Pittsburgh, USA
Works number:	7420
Built:	1942
Running numbers:	1264 (US Army), 61 (SR), 30061 & DS233 (Both BR)
At Redbridge Wharf:	1962-1967

This locomotive came from Southampton Docks, where it was one of 14 that had replaced the ageing B4 tanks (see Chapter 3), remaining there until its class was replaced by a fleet of diesels in 1962. In September that year, it was condemned at Eastleigh, but avoided the scrap heap by being transferred to departmental stock as No DS233, and sent to Redbridge Sleeper Depot a month later. It remained at Redbridge until once again being replaced by a diesel in March 1967. This time there was no reprieve, and No 30061 was scrapped later that year.

For further details of this locomotive see Chapter 3.

CHAPTER 11

Eling Tramway 1851–1993

In July 1847, the Southampton & Dorset Railway (who amalgamated with the LSWR in the following year) was authorised to build a line from the main railway at Totton to Eling Quay. Agreement with the landowner, Sir John Barker Mill, saw the construction of what was originally called the Eling Branch Railway, completed in 1851. The railway company, having built the first section, connected it to their main line, with Barker Mill hiring a contractor to complete the rest of the route from the boundary of his property to the quayside on the River Test. The system terminated at the Mumford steam rolling flour mill.

The wharf was subsequently used by the LSWR for importing timber for sleepers and other associated track laying materials, until they purchased and developed facilities on the opposite side of the river at Redbridge (see Chapter 10).

Over the ensuing years, the railway company made various improvements and additions to the line, and eventually leased it to Mrs Marianne Vaudrey, who had assumed title to the land in 1871. Under the terms of the lease, the line would revert to LSWR ownership if it became unused for a period of three years.

Towards the end of World War I, the Admiralty gave notice of their intention to use the tramway, and the various premises along it, to store munitions boxes in association with the magazine at Marchwood, but this was never implemented before hostilities ceased, and the operation remained with the lessees.

In 1920, the Anglo Gulf West Indies (AGWI) Oil Company began building a terminal at Fawley (later to become the Esso Refinery), and much of the material used in its construction was transported through Eling, via the tramway, and ferried by sea to Ashlett Creek, where a narrow gauge railway was laid down to receive them. Once the refinery had become established and put into production, traffic flowed in the opposite direction, with coastal tankers carrying oil to Eling, where it was pumped aboard wagons and taken along the tramway for main line distribution. However, this traffic ceased when the Totton to Fawley branch line was opened in 1925.

The firm of Burt, Boulton and Haywood Ltd bought the lease on 25th July 1923, and employed two ageing locomotives, *Benton* (Black Hawthorn No 1099 of 1896) and *Cameronian* (Manning Wardle No 653 of 1877), to

This Eling Quay scene, around the turn of the century, shows Mumford's Mill (left) with rails along the water's edge passing The Anchor public house. (Bert Moody Collection)

work the line, which subsequently saw a number of other businesses connect sidings to the tramway. These included South Western Tar Distilleries, the sawmill of Martin Slater (formerly James Fletcher & Sons) who also dealt in coal and corn, and Spooner & Bailey, who engaged in bone crushing for the manufacture of fertiliser.

Operationally, the railway company locomotives hauled wagons from Totton Goods Yard to a point some 140 yards beyond the High Street level crossing, where the BB&H locos would take over (horses being used prior to 1923).

During the 1930s, the principal commodities being handled at Eling were telegraph poles for BB&H which arrived from Canada and the Baltic, while the South Western Tar Distilleries were producing creosote for railway use – in particular, the sleeper impregnating plant at Redbridge Wharf. After World War II, Spooner's bone yard was replaced by large new fertiliser works built by Fisons Ltd, and considerable repairs were made to the tramway, the work being carried out by the Southern Railway on behalf of BB&H.

Locomotives *Benton* and *Cameronian* were both scrapped in 1950, being replaced by a Barclay engine, No 1290, built in 1912. This was named *Benton II* and carried out its duties single-handedly, apart from the occasional assistance of the yard steam cranes.

By the 1960s, the tramway traffic was still healthy but the reign of *Benton II* came to an end in July 1966, when it was scrapped on site after being replaced by Ruston diesel. A decade later, the Amalgamated Roadstone Corporation (ARC) Ltd had built a large stone processing plant with a new siding which opened in 1973, but their rail movements were undertaken by main-line locomotives, and in the summer of 1975, the BB&H diesel loco was disposed of, leaving just the cranes to do what little work remained on the wharf.

In 1987, Redland Tiles opened a new depot alongside the ARC premises, which also had a rail connection, and the tramway's future looked assured, but the ARC traffic ceased in 1988, and that of Redland's just two years later. During this period, in 1989, BB&H had been taken over by Travis Perkins, and rail operations had long ceased there. Thus, in late 1993, with the tramway having been out of use for three years, the railway authorities took the initiative and enacted the clause in the original lease that allowed closure, and severed the connection to the main line in December that year.

"Benton II " at Burt, Boulton & Haywood's Eling Wharf in the 1960s. (Roger Holmes)

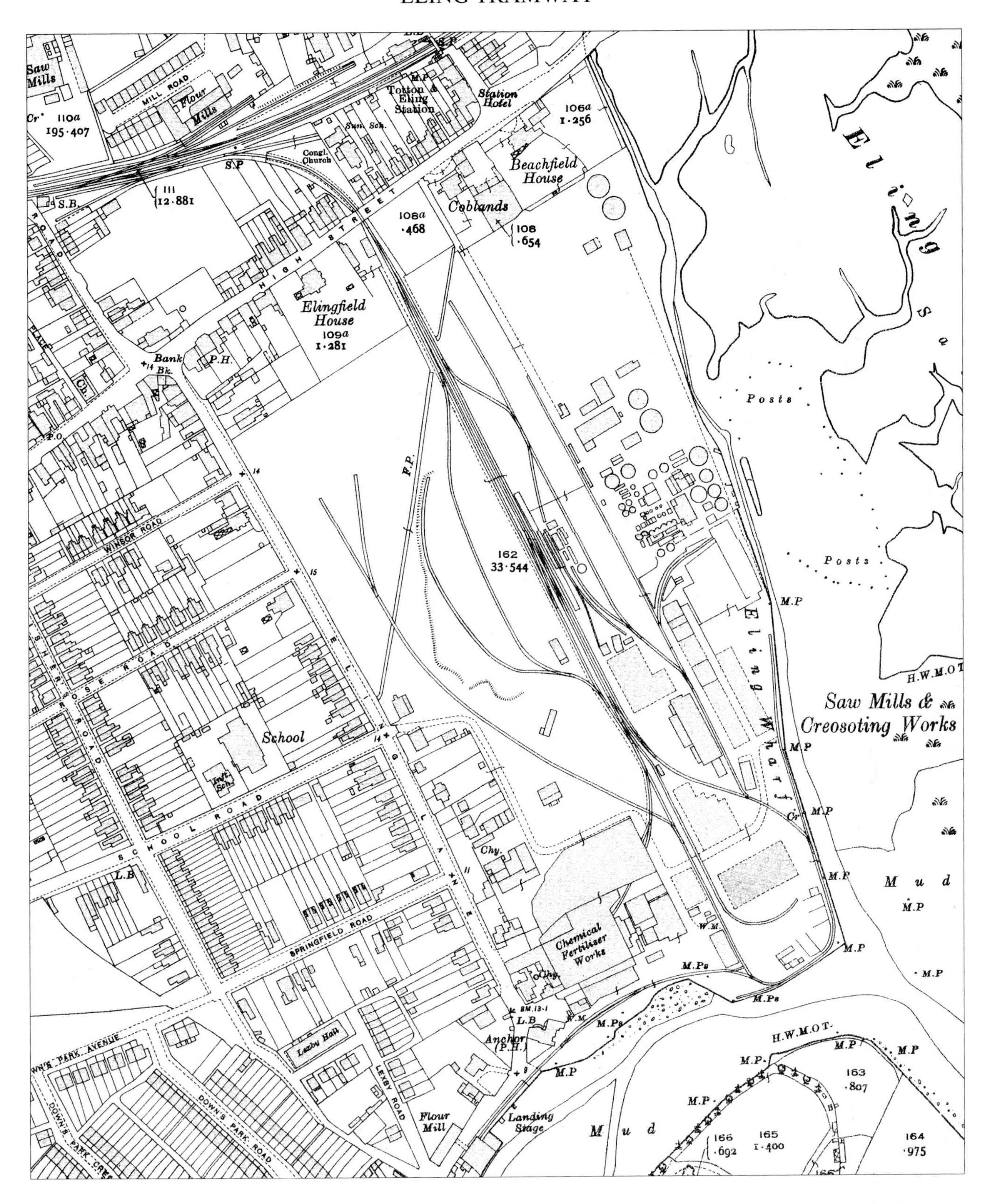

The Eling Tramway in the 1930s. (Reproduced from 1933 Ordnance Survey map with the kind permission of the Ordnance Survey.)

Eling Wharf 0-4-0ST Manning Wardle No 653 *Cameronian*

Name:	(*Cameronian*)
Manufacturer:	Manning, Wardle & Co Ltd, Leeds (rebuilt by Wake)
Works number:	653 (Wake 1774)
Built:	1877
Cylinders:	10in x 16in
Driving wheels:	2ft 9in
Wheelbase:	4ft 9in
Weight:	15ton 0cwt
At Eling Wharf:	1923-1950

Built in August 1877, this locomotive was working on W. Binns' Leen Valley contract from 1895 until 1897, and was at one time employed at Keighley Corporation Gasworks, Yorkshire where it carried the name *Murdock*.

Rebuilt by locomotive dealers John F. Wake at Darlington, and renumbered 1774, it later moved to the Air Ministry at Halton, Bucks as No 122 and was renamed *Cameronian*. It then became RAF No 2, before arriving at Burt, Boulton & Haywood's Totton premises in 1923 (by which time it had lost its name). There, it worked alongside former Woolston Rolling Mills loco *Benton* until both were scrapped by Pollock & Brown of Northam, in around March 1950.

Eling Wharf 0-4-0ST Black Hawthorn No 1099 *Benton*

Name:	*Benton*
Manufacturer:	Black, Hawthorn & Co, Gateshead
Works number:	1099
Built:	1896
At Eling Wharf:	1923-1950

Built in 1896, *Benton* was one of three locos that worked at the Ministry of Munitions Rolling Mills, Woolston (see Chapter 12) during World War I. By 1923, it had moved to the Eling Wharf premises of Burt, Boulton & Haywood Ltd, where it worked alongside Manning Wardle *Cameronian* until both were scrapped by Pollock & Brown at Northam in around March 1950.

For more details of this locomotive see Chapter 12.

Eling Wharf 0-4-0ST Andrew Barclay No 1290 *Benton II*

Name:	*Benton II*
Manufacturer:	Andrew Barclay Sons, Ltd, Kilmarnock
Built:	1912
Works number:	1290
Cylinders:	14in x 22in
Driving wheels:	3ft 6in
Wheelbase:	5ft 6in
At Eling Wharf:	1949-1966

Built in November 1912, *Benton II* was supplied new to the boiler-making firm of Babcock & Wilcox, Renfrew and carried the number 3, working there until sold to dealers George Cohen at Canning Town in April 1948. They, in turn, resold the locomotive to Burt, Boulton & Haywood, where it is thought to have taken the place of the two former BB&H locomotives scrapped in 1950. Here it remained until being replaced by a diesel loco, when it was broken up on site by R.S. Maunder of Southampton in July 1966.

Manning Wardle "Cameronian" in its Royal Air Force days as rebuilt by John Wake. (E. Haigh Collection)

"Benton" placed on temporary rails at Eling Wharf in 1949, prior to being scrapped. "Cameronian" is seen in the background. (G. Alliez)

"Benton II" with steam crane companion at Eling Wharf on 2nd July 1961. (Bert Moody Collection)

Above: Eling Wharf pictured in May 1952. Two of the yard steam cranes mentioned in this chapter can be seen. (Author's Collection)

Left: The South Western Tar Distilleries sidings pictured in 1982. (J.R. Fairman)

CHAPTER 12

Woolston Rolling Mills 1914-1923

At the outbreak of World War I, the Government purchased part of the Western Lawn Estate for the purpose of building a steel-rolling mill. However, the facility was soon converted for the manufacture of munitions.

The depot covered some 82 acres, of which nine were occupied by buildings comprising a factory, foundry, and warehouses. These were served by a large electrical generating station and a gas plant, powered by coal and coke respectively. The fuel was brought in by ships, for which a long jetty was constructed some 800 feet over the mudflats and out to the main channel of the River Itchen.

To transport the coal, coke and heavy materials from ships, a double track standard gauge railway was constructed along the jetty, and round an elevated loop that encircled the power station at a height of some 10ft. A branch led down an incline to ground level along the south side of the main building, where turntables directed the line into the main depot entrances. There was also an internal narrow gauge system for moving materials around the depot in hand-propelled trucks. The rail system was completely isolated with no connection to the main line.

During its short active life, the depot railway employed three locomotives, all of which were 0-4-0STs. The first was a Peckett, No 596 built in 1894, which worked there during the hostilities before being sold to an Admiralty contractor in Grangemouth by the middle of 1918. At some time during its life, this locomotive carried the name *Queen Mary,* but that is not recorded during its stay at Woolston. The Peckett was possibly replaced by *Benton,* a Black Hawthorn & Co engine No 1099 built in 1896, which was subsequently sold to Burt, Boulton and Haywood's Totton works in 1923. Little is known about the third loco, other than it bore the name *Jubilee*, and was noted as being offered for sale during September 1921.

After the war, activities at the depot were run down and the equipment sold off, and various organisations leased parts of the premises, including the Simmonds

A 1950s aerial photograph of the western end of the depot showing part of the elevated section that carried the track around the power station and alongside the main building and the remains of the ramp running down alongside the depot. (Southampton City Archive)

Aircraft Co who produced planes there until 1931. By 1928, the redundant jetty had been converted to carry oil supply pipes from a nearby storage facility for the refuelling of vessels. In 1933, the depot was sold to the electrical switchgear firm of Alan West & Co, who remained there until 1937. By 1940, the Government had bought back the site again for use as a Royal Navy Stores Depot. Thus it remained, until the Admiralty finally sold it off to the local authority in 1987, and a large area was eventually redeveloped for housing, after a lengthy and expensive decontamination of the land.

Two of the locomotives remained there until the 'twenties but there was no further recorded use of the rail system after World War I. Although the power station was knocked down 1956, evidence of the rails remained until at least the 1960s, and the elevated section survived until demolition in 1976. The jetty itself remains today, but is out of use as the oil installation has long since closed.

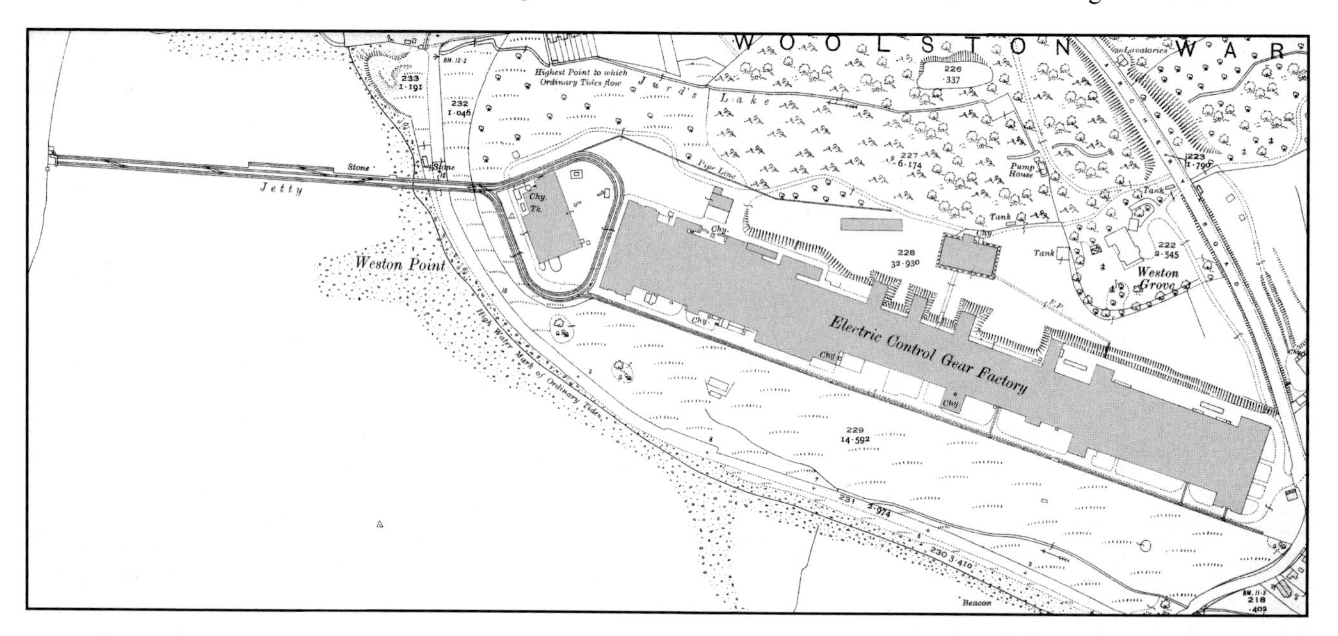

This 1933 map shows the railway layout around the works and out onto the jetty. (Reproduced from 1933 Ordnance Survey map with the kind permission of the Ordnance Survey.)

Woolston Rolling Mills 0-4-0ST Black Hawthorn No 1099 *Benton*

Name:	*Benton*
Manufacturer:	Black Hawthorn & Co, Gateshead
Works number:	1099
Built:	1896
Cylinders:	Diameter: 10in, stroke: unknown
At Woolston Rolling Mills:	1918-1923

Built in 1896, *Benton* had been employed by contractor H.M. Nowell, and was afterwards at the Air Ministry Depot at Halton, Bucks. It then became one of the three locomotives at the Ministry of Munitions Rolling Mills at Woolston. By 1923, it had moved to the premises of Burt, Boulton & Haywood Ltd at Eling Wharf, Totton (see Chapter 11) where it remained until scrapped in March 1950 by Pollock & Brown at Northam.

Woolston Rolling Mills 0-4-0ST *Jubilee*

Name:	*Jubilee*
At Woolston Rolling Mills:	1914-1921

Little is known about *Jubilee*, except that it was one of three locomotives employed by the Ministry of Munitions at Woolston Rolling Mills during World War I, after which it was sold in September 1921, and presumed scrapped.

Woolston Rolling Mills 0-4-0ST Peckett No 596

Name:	(*Queen Mary*)
Manufacturer:	Peckett & Sons, Bristol
Works number:	596
Built:	1894
Cylinders:	12in x 18in
Driving wheels:	2ft 6in
At Woolston Rolling Mills:	1914-1918

Peckett No 596 was delivered new to the Salvation Army Industrial and Land Colony at Hadleigh, Essex in December 1894, where it was employed shunting wagons along a tramway between the brickworks and the barges at Hadleigh Wharf.

Taking the place of a hired loco, it served the colony until the railway closed in 1914, when it moved to the Ministry of Munitions Rolling Mills at Woolston. It is believed to have carried the name *Queen Mary* at some time, and by June 1918, it had moved to Scotland where it was employed by Sir John Jackson Ltd on an Admiralty contract at Grangemouth. Afterwards, it was with dealers J. Pugsley, before being shipped via Swansea in July 1927 to Jackson's contract in Egypt. Following this, it was sold to Topham Jones & Railton, and engaged in works on the Aswan Dam between 1930-1933. No further history is recorded.

Left: This poor quality photo of a Peckett loco at Hadleigh Quay appeared in the Salvation Army Journal "All the World" in 1899, and is assumed to be No 596 ("Queen Mary"). (IRS Collection)

Below: Another poor quality, but interesting photograph of Benton thought to have been taken at Woolston Mills in 1918. (Author's Collection)

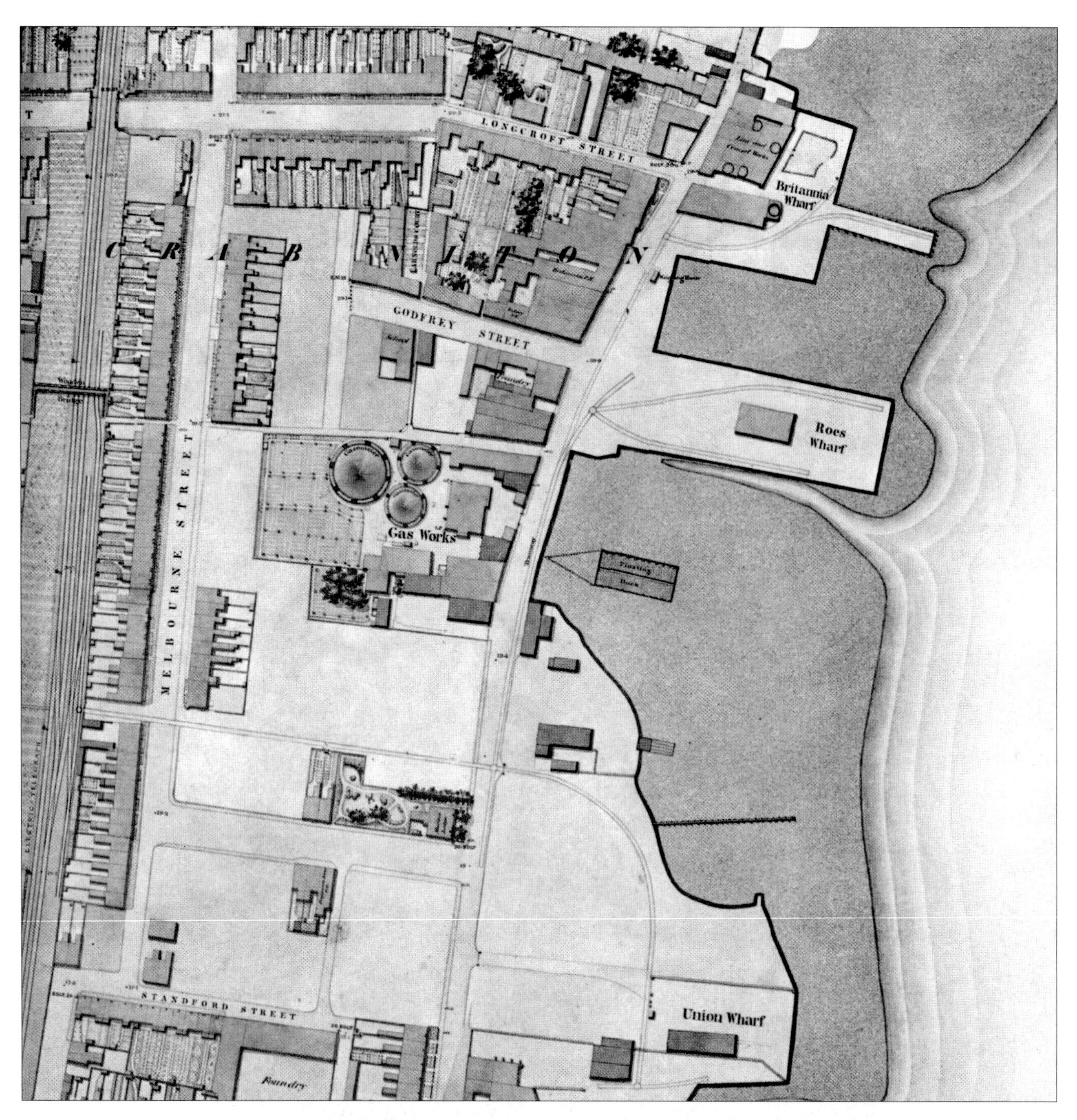

This early Ordnance Survey map shows the Chapel Tramway in its original form as laid down 1843. Note the turntable at the west of Melbourne Street, where the tramway joined the main line sidings and others along Marine Parade running north/south through the middle of the map. (Reproduced from 1846 Ordnance Survey map with the kind permission of the Ordnance Survey.)

CHAPTER 13

The Chapel Tramway 1843–1967

To trace the origins of the tramway, it is necessary to understand how the area evolved from open fields to become one of the most populated areas of the town. By 1800, there had been very little development of the land, most of it being owned by a Mr Charles Godfrey, whose estate occupied much of the area from Northam Road to Chapel Road, and from Love Lane (now St Mary Street) across to the River Itchen. At that time, the only appreciable riverside development was the Chapel Mill and its adjacent quay at Crosshouse. The shoreline to the north of this was mainly mudflats until it reached the ship building yards at Northam.

The first Itchen wharf was established in 1802 by Mr J. Kent who, having leased the site from Godfrey, built what eventually became Britannia Wharf. Other wharves were eventually constructed along the shoreline, and by 1840 the original Kent's Wharf was occupied by a man named Pritchard, who established a cement works and lime kilns on the site. He was also a dealer in bricks and slates, so needed a substantial method of haulage for his goods.

During the previous year, the Northam to Winchester section of the London & Southampton Railway had been completed, and streets of houses had begun to spring up in the Chapel district to accommodate the growing industrial workforce. The docks were under construction, and would soon be finished, and the gasworks was now in place. At that time, ownership of Godfrey's estate had passed to Thomas Bradby, who was approached by Pritchard to build a tramway that would link the wharves to the railway with a connection to the main line at Melbourne Street.

The Chapel Tramway was completed and fully operational by 1843. The route ran from the exchange sidings, just north of the Chapel Road level crossing, across Melbourne Street to Marine Parade, where a turntable directed the tracks either south-east to Union Wharf, or north up Marine Parade to sidings at Roe's Wharf and Britannia Wharf. When the gasworks expanded some 30 years later, further sidings were laid to serve it, the entire system being worked by horses.

The firm of J.R. Wood & Co became established at Burnley Wharf in 1882, and by 1899, had decided to change to locomotive power. At this time, various improvements to the line were carried out, including a realignment of the track at the Melbourne Street junction,

Peckett No 1375 heads across Marine Parade and westwards towards Melbourne Street on 29th June 1957. (I.J. Bovey)

which involved buying four cottages from Bradby and building a new curve across their gardens. The new works replaced the turntable at the exchange sidings, as well others along Marine Parade.

The first locomotive was a second hand 0-4-0ST built by Peckett & Son of Bristol in 1884, works No 438. Having previously been employed at a tinplate works in South Wales, it arrived in February 1899 following an overhaul at its maker's. Woods' change to steam traction had obviously proved a success, as a second loco was ordered. No 923 was delivered new from the works of Andrew Barclay, Kilmarnock, having been built in 1902. A two-road shed was constructed on the boundary of Burnley and Victoria Wharves, and the pair worked the ever growing traffic until 1914, when the Peckett was sold to Blackwell Colliery in Derbyshire, after being replaced by a second new loco, another Peckett, No 1375.

Woods eventually moved their operation northwards to Dibles Wharf, and on 30th June 1926, the tramway and properties were taken over by the Southampton Gas Light and Coke Co Ltd. The gas company formed an operating company named the Chapel Tramway Company Ltd on 31st December 1927, and within a year, annual traffic had risen to 194,000 tons.

Traffic on the line reached its peak in 1942, when 267,000 tons were handled, and business continued to thrive, but by 1954, the annual tonnage had dropped to 43,000 after the Phoenix Coal Company had ceased trading at Phoenix Wharf; in March that year, loco driver John Parker retired after 50 years service. The Gas Board purchased Phoenix Wharf in 1954, but by now, much of the coal coming ashore was conveyed to the coke ovens by a conveyor that ran over a bridge across Marine Parade, or was distributed by road.

The new Peckett had formed a lasting partnership with the established Andrew Barclay until, following the decline in trade, No 923 was scrapped on site by William Forfar Ltd in July 1955 and No 1375 became the sole locomotive for the next five years until the owners decided to replace it with a second Andrew Barclay, No 1398, in November 1960.

The "new" locomotive was, in fact, only a year younger than the Peckett it displaced, having been built in 1915. It had seen service in a variety of locations before ending up at Hilsea Gasworks, prior to transfer to Southampton. By the time it arrived at the Chapel Tramway, a complete overhaul was needed, and this was carried out at Southampton, where many fittings from the Peckett were used; the remains of this loco were sold for scrap in 1961.

No 1398 had been running under the name of *Lord Fisher*, but was without its name and works plates when it arrived at Southampton. With the overhaul completed, it began work as the final tramway loco in 1961, but an immediate problem was that the loco was facing the "wrong way". All the tramway locos had open-backed cabs, which allowed the driver to lean out of the rear of the engine to facilitate coupling wagons with the aid of a hooked pole.

For general operation this meant that the rear of the engine should face the river, but *Lord Fisher* was facing the opposite way. To remedy this, the loco was run down to the British Rail turntable in the loco yard at Western Terrace, just north of the Terminus Station and adjacent to Deanery School. This event was photographed by senior engineer John Fairman, who also rode on the footplate for this historic journey (see picture below).

In August 1961, control of the company was taken

Andrew Barclay No 1398 heads south towards Chapel Road crossing en route to the turntable at Southampton Terminus in 1961. (J.R. Fairman)

over by the Southern Gas Board. Rail traffic continued to decline until it fell to just 3,106 tons in 1966. In those final years, the remaining trade consisted of the occasional two or three vans of cement bags and building materials being delivered to Hooper and Ashby at Britannia Wharf. The Chapel Tramway finally closed on 31st March 1967 with Arthur Budden having carried out the driving duties for the final six years.

The tramway may have closed, but happily the last remaining loco was to be saved, having been purchased by Mr. B.G. Buckfield, and after lying idle in the shed for several weeks, it was taken to Liss military station where it was joined by other locomotives of the Longmoor Trust. During 1974, it followed the procession of engines to Cranmore, where it is still in regular use on the East Somerset Railway.

The rails along Marine Parade were lifted soon after the tramway closure to allow for road widening, and removal of the section through the gasworks followed quickly afterwards. The shed and sidings on the wharves had all disappeared by 1975, when many of the quayside areas were resurfaced for the sand and ballast firms now operating there. Long after the houses in Melbourne Street were demolished, the curve to the exchange sidings became hidden by weeds and remained undiscovered until local archaeologists excavated the area in 1974. After that, the only visible evidence of the tramway's existence was the Melbourne Street crossing where two rusty metal rails lay embedded in the concrete until their removal as late as 1990. Thus ended a small but important chapter in Southampton's railway history, as this once essential local industrial system became just a memory.

By the late 1970s much of the gasworks south of the former Longcroft Street had been dismantled. The vacant land was developed as the Central Industrial Estate, which now stands between the boundaries of Melbourne Street, Standford Street and Marine Parade. The main area of the works north of Longcroft Street became a storage and parking area, until eventually becoming the new home of Southampton Football Club as the St. Mary's Stadium in 2001.

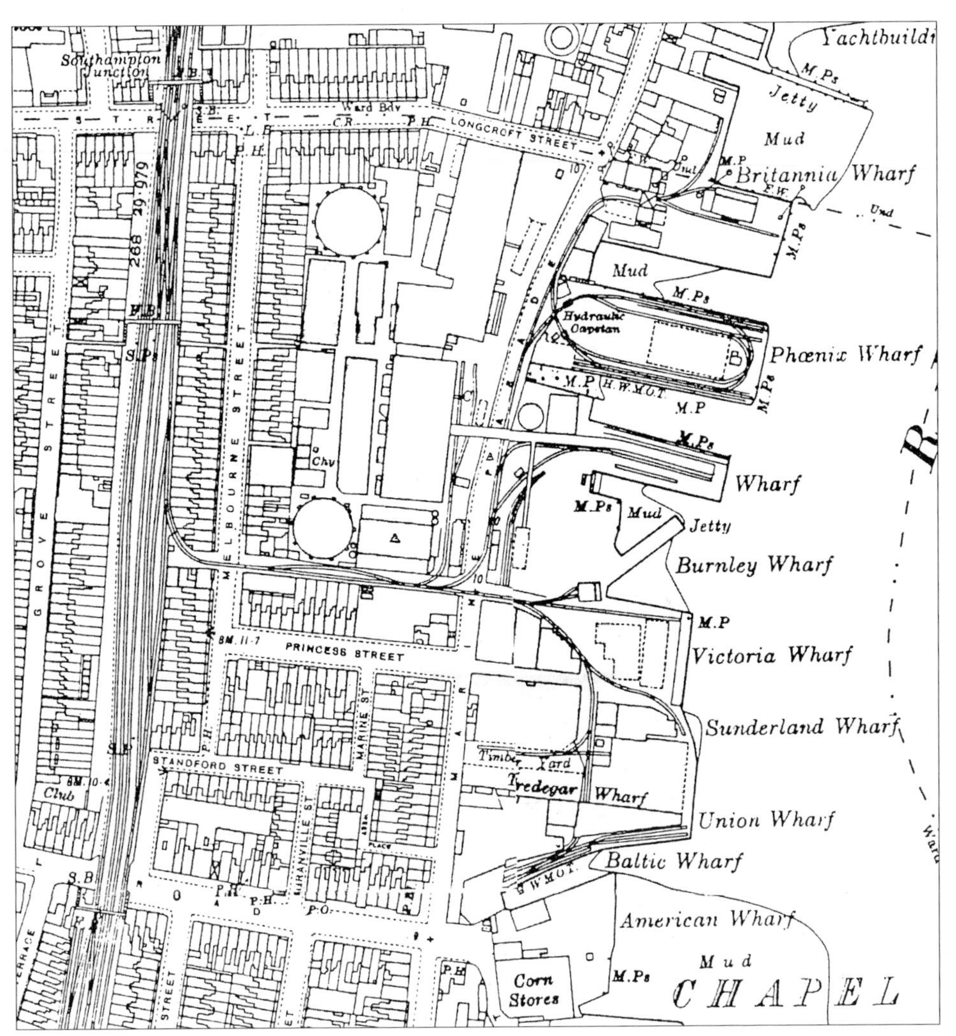

The Chapel Tramway at its full extent in the 1930s. (Reproduced from 1933 Ordnance Survey map with the kind permission of the Ordnance Survey.)

Chapel Tramway 0-4-0ST Peckett No 438

Manufacturer:	Peckett & Sons, Bristol
Works number:	438
Built:	1884
Cylinders:	10in x 14in
Driving wheels:	2ft 6in
Wheelbase:	5ft 0in
At the Chapel Tramway:	1899-1914

Peckett class M3 No 438 was delivered on September 1884 to the Ynispenllwch Tinplate Works at Glais where, in May 1885, its boiler exploded. Peckett's repaired the damage, and fitted a new copper firebox. The tin works were closed and dismantled in 1897, and No 438 was not heard of again until 1898, when the Clayton Tinplate Co Ltd, Pontardulais, Glamorgan returned it to Peckett. It was then sold to J.R. Wood and Co Ltd at Burnley Wharf, Southampton in February 1899, where it remained until purchased by the Blackwell Colliery Co Ltd, Derbyshire in March 1914. No 498 is then thought to have been purchased by Thomas W. Ward Ltd in April 1918, and scrapped the following September at the company's works at Charlton, Sheffield.

Chapel Tramway 0-4-0ST Andrew Barclay No 923

Manufacturer:	Andrew Barclay & Sons, Kilmarnock
Works number:	923
Built:	1902
Cylinders:	10in x 18in
Driving wheels:	3ft 0in
Wheelbase:	5ft 0in
At the Chapel Tramway:	1902-1955

Supplied new from the makers to the tramway in 1902, where it worked alongside elderly Peckett No 438. It was eventually taken out of service, and scrapped on site by local firm William Forfar Ltd in July 1955.

Chapel Tramway 0-4-0ST Peckett No 1375

Manufacturer:	Peckett & Sons, Bristol
Works number:	1375
Built:	1914
Cylinders:	10in x 15in
Driving wheels:	2ft 9in
Wheelbase:	5ft 0in
At the Chapel Tramway:	1914-1961

No 1375 was delivered new to the tramway in 1914, replacing the earlier Peckett (No 438). Here it worked with No 923 until that locomotive was scrapped in 1955. Afterwards, it operated as the sole motive power until, following the arrival of *Lord Fisher* in November 1960, it was broken up in July the following year.

Peckett M3 class locomotive design showing how No 438 would have looked.

Andrew Barclay No 923 poses at the Melbourne Street crossing in September 1949. (G. Alliez)

Peckett No 1375 on the exchange sidings at the rear of Melbourne Street. (Author's Collection)

Chapel Tramway 0-4-0ST Andrew Barclay No 1398

Name:	(*Lord Fisher*)
Manufacturer:	Andrew Barclay & Sons, Kilmarnock
Works number:	1398
Built:	1915
Cylinders:	10in x 18in
Driving wheels:	3ft 0in
Wheelbase:	5ft 0in
Working pressure:	120psi
Weight :	15ton 0cwt
At the Chapel Tramway:	1961-1967

Andrew Barclay No 1398 was supplied new to the Kingsnorth Airship Station in Kent in September 1915, moving from there to the Royal Aircraft Establishment, Farnborough, Hants. In January 1942, it was moved to the Yorktown (Camberley) & District Gas & Electricity Co, where it carried the name *Lord Fisher*, and worked until 1949 when it was transferred to Blackwater Gasworks. Then, in August 1956, came another move, this time to Hilsea Gasworks, Portsmouth. There, it eventually became surplus to requirements, and was partially dismantled before being sent to Southampton in November 1960 as a replacement for Peckett No 1375. Running without its name, in early 1961, it became the last locomotive to work the tramway until its closure on 31st March 1967, when it was taken out of service and stored in its shed.

By October that year, it had been purchased by Mr B.G. Buckfield, and moved to the Longmoor Military Railway for preservation. In June 1972, it was transferred to the East Somerset Railway, where it once again took the name *Lord Fisher* and currently enjoys an active retirement.

Barclay No 1398 ("Lord Fisher") on its final working day at the tramway in 1967. (Author's Collection)

CHAPTER 14

The "Bull's Run" Line (Dibles Wharf) 1869–1987

The company of Joseph Bull & Sons was associated with much early railway construction in the Southampton area, and in the late 1860s they built their own tramway to connect their works at Belvidere Wharf to the main London & South Western Railway at Northam. In fact, they also built Northam station a little later.

The single track line joined exchange sidings just south of the Northam Road bridge, and curved south-eastwards to Britannia Road (then unnamed), which it crossed on the level, heading eastwards over a weighbridge and to the north of stables at Belvidere Road. At this point, the line ran directly across the road and into the works. Not surprisingly, the line took the name "Bull's Run" because of its association with its builders. In its earliest days, there was also a branch that ran southwards, along the east side of Britannia Road to a wharf that was once the yacht building yard of Summers & Payne (opposite the present-day gas company flats).

Bulls had moved away by the turn of century, and a pencil note revision on an 1881 Ordnance Survey map indicates the whole line as a "Disused Railway". The Powell Duffryn Steam Coal Co had taken over the wharf premises by that time, and by 1910, had successfully applied for the track to be doubled in order to handle its incoming coal shipments. Throughout this period, there is no record of them owning a locomotive, and it is assumed their trains would have been worked by horses or railway company engines.

James Dible and Sons were shipbuilders occupying the adjacent Belvidere Shipyard, which eventually became known as Dibles Wharf, but in July 1926, the site was taken over by coal merchants J.R. Wood & Co, who had

This aerial photograph taken in 1953 shows the general layout Dibles Wharf after reconstruction works. One of the Peckett locos can just be seen with two wagons near the gate. (Author's Collection)

moved upriver from Burnley Wharf, where they had been principal users of the Chapel Tramway (see Chapter 13).

On arrival at Dibles Wharf, Woods sought a link to the adjacent "Bull's Run", and a connection was made, with a new line running north-east across Belvidere Road, and providing various sidings around the wharf. Woods had introduced locomotive power to the Chapel Tramway in 1899, and upon setting up at Dibles, took possession of ex-Southampton Dock Co saddle tank *Bretwalda* in November 1926. Despite being built in 1878, *Bretwalda* gave good service until scrapped in September 1935. when replaced by Peckett No 1638 named *Bristol*. This was another 0-4-0ST that had been built in 1923, and arrived from the Barnsley Gas Company after an overhaul at its manufacturer's works.

Woods were succeeded by Southern Wharves on 16th February 1940, and the locomotive was joined by another Peckett (No 2128), which was delivered new in 1952. The pair then worked for a decade until operation of the wharf was transferred to P.D. Fuels (Corrall) Ltd, on 1st October 1962. The wharf was now a major distribution centre where, as well as the seaborne trade, coal was arriving in trains of hopper wagons via the main line. Within a year, a replacement was being sought for *Bristol*, and once again, a former docks loco made its way to Dibles Wharf in December 1963.

B4 class No 30096 was surplus to requirements at BR, and now gained a new lease of life at Northam. Having lost its original name of *Normandy* after leaving the docks in 1947, it was renamed *Corrall Queen* by its new owners. At the same time, *Bristol* was scrapped by the Brooklyn Engineering Co at Chandlers Ford.

The comparatively young Peckett No 2128 lasted only two more years before being sent to the nearby scrapyard of Pollock & Brown Ltd in September 1965, where it remained until being broken up in May the following year.

At the time, Corrall's depot at Hamworthy, Poole, employed two most handsome saddle tanks built in 1949 by Robert Stephenson & Hawthorn as Nos 7544 and 7645, bearing the respective names *Bonnie Prince Charlie* and *Western Pride*. When the Northam location needed another locomotive, the former was nominated to make the journey along the south coast as a replacement for the Peckett, with the possibility of its sister engine joining forces again in the near future.

Unfortunately, after its arrival in September 1965,

"Corrall Queen" enjoys a spell of rest at Dibles Wharf on 20th July 1968. (R.K. Blencowe Collection)

Bonnie Prince Charlie was found to lack sufficient power to handle the heavy trains of hopper wagons, and was soon relegated to little more than standby status. *Corrall Queen* soldiered on and *Bonnie Prince Charlie* was eventually replaced by a diesel loco in February 1968, when it was finally taken out of service. Happily, the diminutive Prince was saved for preservation by the Salisbury Locomotive Trust, and a year later, was transferred to the Didcot Railway Centre where it still resides. On a sadder note, *Western Pride* also made the journey to Northam in March 1966, but only to be broken up at the nearby scrap yard of Pollock & Brown.

Corrall Queen became the last steam locomotive to work the "Bull's Run", as the new era began at Dibles with the arrival of the diesel engine in February 1968, after which the 1893-built veteran shared duties and saw out her time until retired from service in 1972, when it was sold to the Bulleid Preservation Society.

Two more diesels were brought to Dibles before the line's eventual closure in 1987, when "King Coal" had fallen from grace as the modern world turned to other forms of fuel. Corralls relocated, and the yard diversified by handling other products that were transported by road. The connection to the main line was severed two years later, and with almost all traces of track now removed, the most visible remaining evidence being the walled "cutting" through today's remnants of the gasworks to Britannia Road, where the rails have long been lifted and road vehicles are stored on the old track bed.

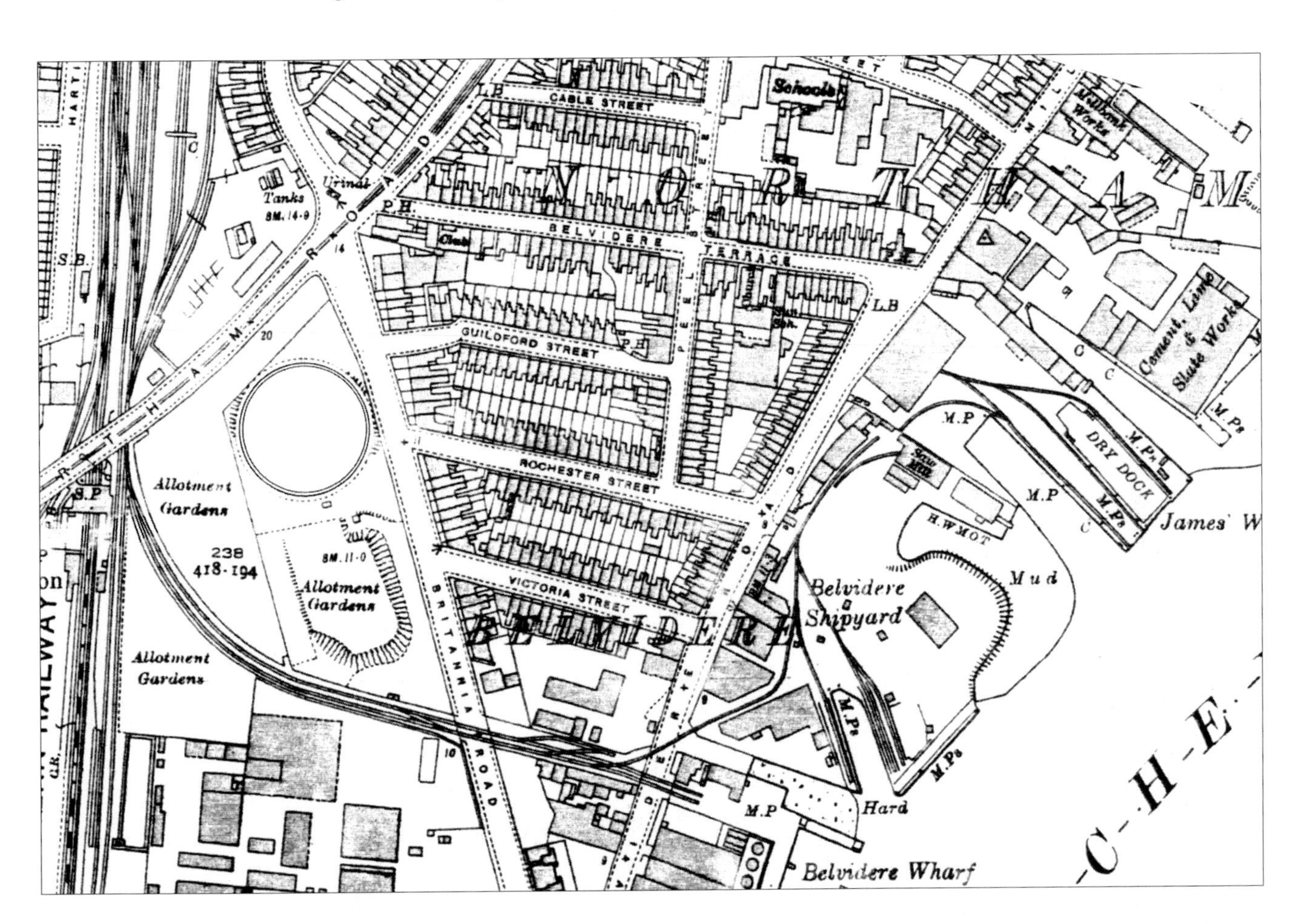

The line to Dibles Wharf in 1933. By then, the original tracks into Belvidere Wharf were out of use. The map also shows tracks around the shipyard at James' Wharf, but there is no evidence of these having been connected to the main system. (Reproduced from 1933 Ordnance Survey map with the kind permission of the Ordnance Survey.)

Dibles Wharf 0-4-0ST Vulcan No 2174 *Bretwalda*

Manufacturer:	Vulcan Foundry Ltd, Newton-le-Willows, Lancashire
Built:	1878
Running Numbers:	408, 0408, (both LSWR), E0408 (SR)
At Dibles Wharf:	1926-1935

Former Southampton Dock Co locomotive *Bretwalda* came to Dibles Wharf when sold by the Southern Railway in November 1926. This was the first known locomotive to work the line following the arrival of J.R. Wood & Co, who had taken over the wharf some four months earlier. The ageing veteran was finally cut up in September 1935, when it was replaced by Peckett No 1638 *Bristol.*

For full details of this loco see Chapter 1.

Dibles Wharf 0-4-0ST Peckett No 1638 *Bristol*

Name:	*Bristol*
Manufacturer:	Peckett & Sons, Bristol
Works number:	1638
Built:	1923
Cylinders:	12in x 18in
Driving wheels:	3ft ½in
Wheelbase:	5ft 3in
At Dibles Wharf:	1935-1963

Bristol was supplied new to the Barnsley Gas Company, Yorkshire, in October 1923, and worked there until moving to Dibles Wharf in September 1935, where it replaced the veteran Vulcan *Bretwalda.* It was later joined by another Peckett (No 2128) in 1952, and the pair worked the wharf lines until *Bristol* was replaced by another ex-Southampton Docks locomotive, B4 class No 30096, in December 1963. On the arrival of the B4, it was sold to the Brooklyn Engineering Co Ltd, Chandlers Ford, and scrapped in the same month.

Dibles Wharf 0-4-0ST Peckett No 2128

Manufacturer:	Peckett & Sons, Bristol
Works number:	2128
Built:	1952
Cylinders:	12in x 20in
Driving wheels:	3ft ½in
Wheelbase:	5ft 3in
At Dibles Wharf:	1952–1965

Peckett No 2128 was built in December 1951, and arrived new from the makers in early 1952, joining the already established Peckett, *Bristol.* The two combined duties at Dibles until the latter was replaced by ex-BR class B4 *Corrall Queen* in December 1963. No 2128 survived until September 1965, when it was sold for scrap to the nearby firm of Pollock and Brown at Northam, and was broken up in May the following year, its place being taken by *Bonnie Prince Charlie*, which had arrived from P.D. Fuels' other depot at Hamworthy Quay.

Former Southampton Dock Company loco "Bretwalda" gains a new lease of life at Dibles Wharf. (F. Jones)

"Bristol" crossing Belvidere Road to enter Dibles Wharf on 11th October 1955. (Colin Boocock)

Peckett No 2128 at Dibles Wharf yard circa 1960. (TLP Collection)

Dibles Wharf Ex-LSWR 0-4-0T *Corrall Queen*

Name:	*Corrall Queen* (*Normandy*)
Manufacturer:	LSWR, Nine Elms Works
Built:	1893
Running Numbers:	96 (LSWR), 30096 (BR and P D Fuels)
At Dibles Wharf:	1963-1972

This LSWR veteran was in general BR service at Eastleigh when sold in October 1963 to P.D. Fuels at Dibles Wharf. Having previously been named *Normandy* during its years at Southampton Docks, the new owners called it *Corrall Queen* (Corralls Ltd. being a division of the parent company), but retained its BR number on the smoke box door. "The Queen" became the mainstay of the wharf traffic when Peckett No 2128 was scrapped in 1965, and its replacement, *Bonnie Prince Charlie*, was reduced to standby status. However, its own role was reduced on the arrival of the company's first diesel locomotive in February 1968, and rather than have it suffer the same fate as their earlier locos, the owners sought to send the old girl into preservation. In December 1972, the loco passed to the Bulleid Preservation Society, who found it a new home on the Bluebell Railway where, once again in its original guise as *Normandy*, it enjoys an active retirement.

For full details of this locomotive see Chapter 2 and the illustration on page 146.

Dibles Wharf 0-4-0ST RS&H No 7544 *Bonnie Prince Charlie*

Name:	*Bonnie Prince Charlie*
Manufacturer:	Robert Stephenson & Hawthorns Ltd, Newcastle-on-Tyne
Works Number:	7544
Built:	1949
Cylinders:	10in x 15in
Driving wheels	2ft 10in
Wheelbase	5ft 0in
Weight	17ton 0cwt
At Dibles Wharf:	1965-1969

Built in August 1949, *Bonnie Prince Charlie* was one of a pair of immaculate locomotives based at P.D. Fuels' depot on Poole's Hamworthy Quay, the other being *Western Pride*. *Bonnie Prince Charlie* arrived at Dibles in September 1965, but was found to lack the necessary power to cope with the large hopper wagons, and was soon relegated to standby status behind ex-B4 class *Corrall Queen*, the company's existing engine. "Charlie's" short reign ended in February 1969 when, having been replaced by a diesel loco, it was purchased by Great Western Preservations Ltd, and taken by road to the Didcot Railway Centre where it remains today, restored to its former glory.

"Bonnie Prince Charlie" at Dibles Wharf on 20th July 1968. (R.K. Blencowe)

CHAPTER 15

Northam Quay Tramway 1840-1984

From Northam Quay, early tracks were laid in about 1840 to carry coal shipments from vessels to the nearby coke ovens, just south of the modern day Mount Pleasant crossing. In its earliest form, the tramway ran as a double track from the exchange sidings at the coke ovens across to what was the marshy foreshore of the River Itchen (nowadays the north end of Radcliffe Road). From there, it continued eastwards along the shoreline, before a level crossing carried a single track over Northam Road prior to it curving northwards onto Northam Quay.

The firm of Dixon & Cardus was importing materials for its nearby mill, which produced linseed oil and artificial manure. Sidings were laid from the quay into their premises by 1855, and a decade later, the tramway had been extended further from a junction east of Northam Road to the shipyard of Day, Summers & Co at Northam Ironworks. Along the new route, connections were made to the sawmills and timber sheds at Drivers Wharf. There was also a branch into an adjacent corn store at Northam Steam Mill.

By 1897, the Le Dansk margarine factory of Auguste Pellerine had been established alongside the line on the site of an old soap and candle works to the south of the timber sheds. At Northam Quay, they imported animal fat from Paris abattoirs which was carried in plaster-sealed barrels for processing at their works. As with most such operations of the day, the whole system was worked by horses until motive power was considered after the turn of the century.

By 1910, an additional siding was laid near the Radcliffe Road crossing to serve Mount Pleasant Wharf.

Dixon & Cardus employed two locomotives, which were housed in a shed near the Ship Inn. The first was *Eva,* a Manning Wardle 0-4-0ST No 213 dating from 1866 that had previously worked for contractors Lucas and Aird before arriving at Northam in 1911. *Eva* remained in service until 1920, when she was sold to Petters Ltd, Yeovil, following the arrival of *Nicholson*, a John Fowler 0-4-2T locomotive (No 10978) built in 1907.

Nicholson had previously been at the Royal Artillery establishment in Lydd, Kent, where it ran as War Department No 1882 before moving to Northam in 1919. Its duties at Dixon & Cardus continued until it was taken out of service and scrapped in 1934 after the closure of the

Northam Quay with the timber shed of Drivers Wharf beyond, circa 1900. (Southampton City Archive)

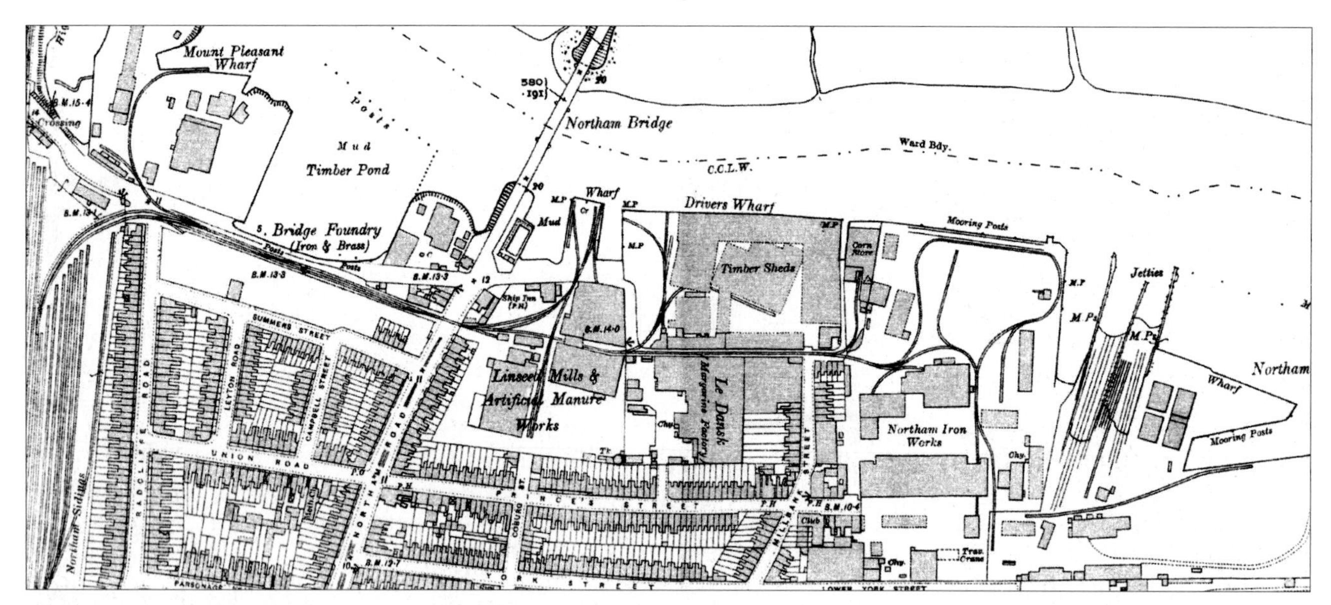

company. The remaining line and the premises along it were subsequently worked by a petrol-driven locomotive based at the Le Dansk factory.

During 1953-4, the iron river bridge, just to the west of the quay, was rebuilt, and around that time, the Southern Independent Television studios were constructed on the old foreshore. These works necessitated a rerouting of the line further to the north, where it now passed between the TV studio buildings and under the new bridge.

The Le Dansk factory eventually closed around 1957, by which time rail traffic to most of the other premises had also ceased. From that time onwards, scrap merchants Pollock Brown and Co, (who had taken over the old iron works) became the principal operators, using a succession of diesels to work the line until it finally closed in 1984.

Above: Dixon & Cardus workers pose for the camera circa 1920. (Southampton City Archive)

Opposite page, top: The Northam Quay Railway at its peak in the 1930s. (Reproduced from 1933 Ordnance Survey map with the kind permission of the Ordnance Survey.)

Opposite page, bottom: A rare glimpse of "Eva" shunting on Northam Quay. (Southampton City Archive)

Manning Wardle No 213 "Eva" of 1866 at Petters Yard at Yeovil in 1934. (B.D. Stoyel)

Northam Quay 0-4-0ST Manning Wardle No 213 *Eva*

Name:	*Eva*
Manufacturer:	Manning Wardle & Co Ltd, Leeds
Works number:	213 (736)
Built:	1866
Cylinders:	9½in x 14in
Driving wheels:	2ft 8in
Wheelbase:	4ft 9in
Weight:	11ton 0cwt
At Northam Quay:	1911-1920

Eva began life in August 1866, when she was delivered to contractors William Moss, Crewe, and given the name *Stafford.* Having undergone a complete rebuild by her makers in January 1879, and renumbered 736, she was sent to another contracting firm of Lucas & Aird, Bristol in July that year, where she carried the name *Boyne.* She had another major overhaul in the 1890s at the engineering firm of P. Baker at Cardiff.

Lucas & Aird then sold her to Dixon & Cardus at Northam Quay in 1911, where she was again renamed as *Eva* while working the traffic from vessels into the company's mill. The ageing loco was eventually replaced by *Nicholson* in 1919, and sold to Petters Westland Works at Yeovil in 1920. *Eva* worked the Petters sidings until 1931, when she was replaced by a diesel loco, and relegated to the role of standby engine, making only an occasional appearance over the next few years. The end finally came in 1935, when she was last seen loaded aboard a wagon on her way to the scrapyard.

Northam Quay 0-4-2T John Fowler No 10978 *Nicholson*

Name:	*Nicholson*
Manufacturer:	John Fowler & Co, Leeds
Works number:	10978
Built:	1907
Cylinders:	10in x 16in
At Northam Quay:	1919-1934

Previously at the Royal Artillery Depot, Lydd, Kent, where it served as War Department No 1882, *Nicholson* arrived at the Northam premises of Dixon & Cardus in 1919, displacing the ageing Manning Wardle saddle tank *Eva.* It remained there until replaced by a Muir Hill petrol locomotive in 1934, and was scrapped soon afterwards.

"Nicholson" at the Northam works of Dixon & Cardus. Its successor lurks behind. (IRS Collection)